Dorothy Denton's Diary

THE EVERYDAY LIFE OF AN EDWARDIAN GIRL

by
Cedric Parcell

Highgate Publications (Beverley) Ltd.
1992

© Copyright Cedric Parcell 1992

Published by Highgate Publications (Beverley) Ltd.
24 Wylies Road, Beverley. HU17 7AP.
Telephone (0482) 866826

Printed and Typeset in 10 on 11pt Plantin by
Colourspec, Unit 7, Tokenspire Park,
Hull Road, Woodmansey, Beverley. HU17 0TB.
Telephone (0482) 864264

ISBN 0-948929-62-6

British Library Cataloguing in Publication Data

Parcell, Cedric
 Dorothy Denton's Diary: Everyday Life of
 an Edwardian Girl
 I. Title
 942.830823092

   ISBN 0-948929-62-6

ACKNOWLEDGEMENTS

It would have been impossible for me to have written this book without assistance and I am grateful to the many people who have co-operated by offering me their personal recollections and the loan of various books, photographs and family possessions.

Much of the material I have used has been obtained from newspaper files and I should like to record my appreciation of the help given by Jill Crowther in the Local Studies Library, Hull, through whom I had access to the *Hull Daily Mail* and *Hull Times* archives, and for the provision of most of the photographs used in this book. The staff at the Beverley and Bridlington Libraries were equally helpful.

As well as members of my family, my brother, Ian Parcell, and cousin Arnold Silvester, and Bunty Barugh, many people, previously unknown to me, came forward with information: Bill Westoby of Anlaby was a mine of information on East Riding villages; Alan Kerr provided background to Hull's theatres and cinemas; Keith Sinclair on Hull schools; Miss C.L. Scholes on St. Matthew's Church; R. Farrah sent me interesting recollections of old Newington; Nicholas Evans allowed me to use picture postcards from his collection; whilst Robin Sharpe provided details of the Great Bridlington Storm of 1871.

Sue Franklin, Sheila Lambert and Eileen Cussons helped with information on old Newington families, and to Albert Theede of Flensburg I owe special thanks for the tracing of Dorothy's pre-war German sweetheart. Rex Alston, now in his 90s, confirmed his recollections of cricket at the Circle.

The Hull companies mentioned in the book have been most helpful and I acknowledge with thanks the receipt of the book, *Twenty-one and a half Bishop lane*, by Ralph Davis, the history of J.H. Fenner & Co. Ltd; Gordon Stephenson of Reckitt & Colman allowed me access to the company archives and supplied photographs, and Miss D.M. Mitchell, archivist of General Accident, took considerable pains to answer my questions on the history of the Yorkshire Insurance Company.

I should also like to thank Miss J.M. Wraight of the Guildhall Library, London, for information from Lloyd's records on the s.s. *Delphic*; and finally a special thank you to my wife Beryl for patiently reading my manuscript and correcting my punctuation and spelling errors.

October, 1992   Cedric Parcell

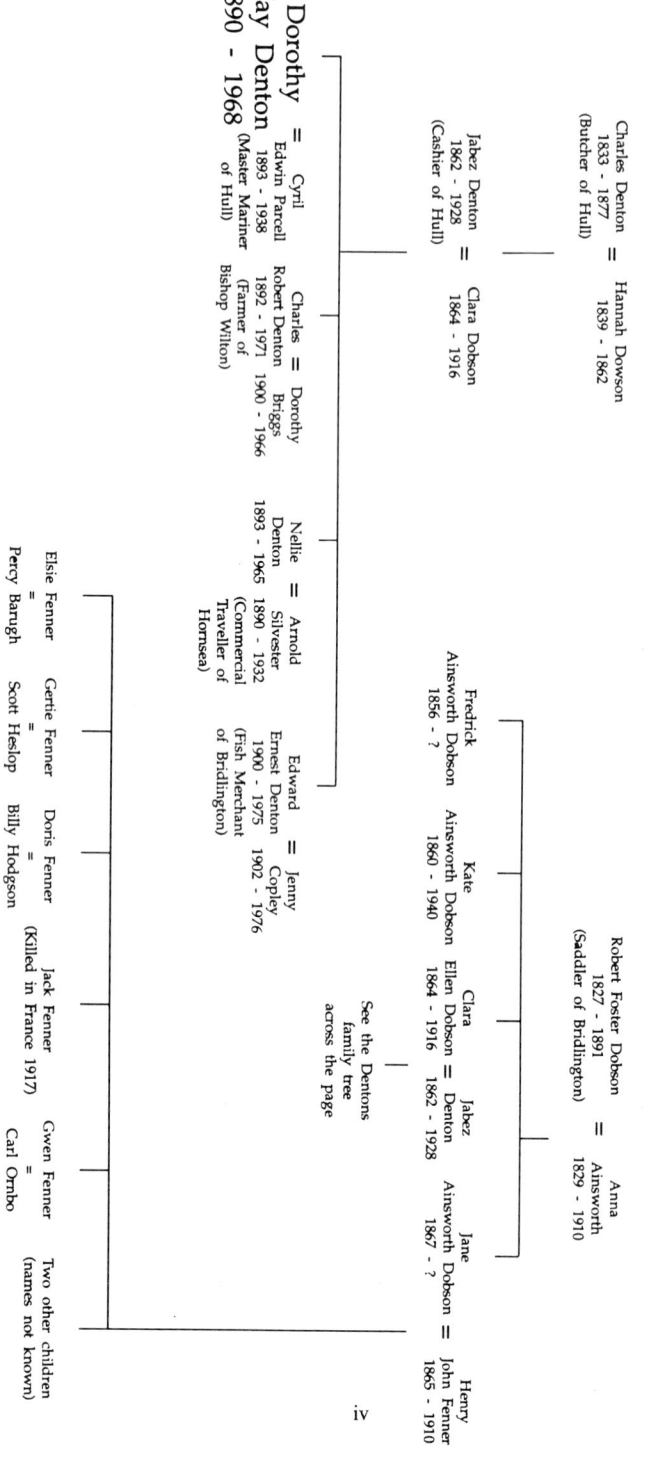

DOROTHY DENTON'S DIARY

Reading other people's diaries has a fascination which cannot be denied, especially when the writer is well-known to the reader. Dorothy May Denton, my mother, kept a diary in the years before the First World War, those carefree days so nostalgically recalled as a golden age before the world went mad. She was born on 7 June 1890 and lived her teenage years through the reign of Edward VII, a typical middle-class girl of the Edwardian era.

Dorothy was 16 when she started to write her diary; she did not record the events of every single day, nor did she reveal to us her innermost thoughts. In fact, much of what she wrote may seem trivial and inconsequential. But read now, after an interval of more than 80 years, the events she confided to her diary offer a fascinating picture of life in an age which very few people can recall. Because not everything she wrote would interest today's reader, I have made no attempt to reproduce the diary in its entirety; I have picked out some of the more interesting entries, and tried to explain them against the background of life in Edwardian England. My mother loved to talk of her younger days, and much of the detail in this book comes from conversations recalled over the years. For the rest, I have relied on contemporary newspaper accounts; the *Hull Daily Mail* and other local newspapers had the space in those days to report local events at length, employing the long-winded and flowery prose of the day. Despite their verbosity, many of these reports still make fascinating reading, painting a word-picture of life as it was lived in Hull and the East Riding of Yorkshire before the First World War.

Writing now, near the end of the century, I find it hard to believe that I am only one generation removed from the scene I describe. The changes that have taken place since 1922 have been prodigious. But I was born close enough to Edwardian times to recognise some aspects of it that had hardly changed. It is not difficult for me to imagine Hull as it was in the first decade of the century, with its gas-lit, cobbled streets, horse-drawn vehicles, its theatres, cinemas, cafés and places of entertainment, as well as its rows of mean terraced houses and the respectable villas of Newington. They had by no means all disappeared in the Twenties and Thirties of my boyhood.

The world that Dorothy knew as a girl would seem a small one to today's much travelled generation. She wrote about her school, the theatres and music-halls, the band concerts, the exhibitions, West Park, Hull Fair, holidays at Bridlington and Filey, and, of course, her family and friends. What else would you expect a teenage girl to write about in her diary? Her innermost secrets, if she had any, she kept to herself. That they were happy days I have no doubt, for she always spoke of her childhood as a golden era. Nowhere in her diary does she complain about anything – 'had a lovely time', 'enjoyed it all immensely', 'simply grand', are the expressions she most often uses. Everything in Dorothy's garden was lovely, and she was luckier than most. The majority of Hull's citizens looked out on to vistas of terrace-ends and dingy back-yards rather than on to flower-beds and neat lawns. The gap between rich and poor was wider, and middle-class families were much fewer in number in 1906 than they are today.

So, to balance Dorothy's accounts of theatre evenings, trips to the country, and long seaside holidays, I have thought it right to include accounts of how the less fortunate managed – the elderly poor, or the inmates of the workhouse. I have tried to shed light on the moral climate of the day: for example, the narrow-minded carping of theatre critics, the sanctimonious opinions of self-appointed judges of public morals, the condescension of the middle-classes towards their domestic servants, the prissy indignation over what we would today consider mild vulgarity, the snobbish superiority of the amateur over the professional sportsman.

But there is much to be said in favour of Edwardian standards. Families like the Dentons knew what they could, and could not, afford. There was nobody then persuading them to live on credit. If they lacked motor cars, television sets and holidays abroad, neither did they have the worry of how to pay for such pleasures. Family life was solid, and father's word was law. Divorce for all but the most wealthy was out of the question, and parents taught their children the difference between right and wrong. School-children sat obediently at their desks learning to spell and recite multiplication tables, with the threat of the stick if they did not behave themselves. Men in cloth caps and mufflers went to football matches in their thousands, and there was never a moment's trouble. Law-abiding citizens could walk the streets safely.

This was the confident golden age about which Dorothy wrote in her diary. Like children playing on the sands of her beloved Bridlington, blissfully unaware of the storm clouds gathering, Dorothy and her generation innocently watched the first years of the new century unfold.

THE DIARY - 1906

Commenced at Aston High School for Girls on Monday September 24th, 1906.

A big day in Dorothy's life, and this was the day on which she began to keep her diary; she wrote it regularly for the next five years, sometimes recording life's trivialities, and sometimes important events – like commencing at Aston High School for Girls.

She had left Boulevard Higher Grade School that summer. Her schooldays had been happy ones, and she made many friendships at the Boulevard – some of them lasting a lifetime. She wasn't an outstanding scholar, but she was good at the subjects she enjoyed, and in her last term won an English prize, a leather-bound copy of *Dombey and Son*.

In those days most girls left elementary school at 13 or 14. Dorothy was one of the few who carried on at secondary school to 16, and her younger sister, Nellie, who was to become a teacher, stayed on even longer. But education for girls beyond 'higher-grade' to university was comparatively rare, and the few who achieved it gained scant reward, for most universities would not award a degree to a woman. So on leaving school a girl like Dorothy had few alternatives open to her. She could stay at home and help mother until she married, find a congenial job (becoming easier now that offices and banks were employing more girls), or continue her education at one of those private schools where she could be instructed in one or other of the arts, and learn to be a young lady at the same time. Father offered her this latter choice.

Aston High School for Girls on Anlaby Road occupied two large converted houses at the corner of Arlington Street. It had been established as a girls' boarding school back in the 1890s by a Miss Sarah Jane Aston. It advertised itself in the *Hull Daily Mail* as a 'superior school with boarding arrangements under the direct supervision of the Principal'. In 1906 the Principal was Mrs. G.A. Lambert. The prospectus advised that 'pupils are prepared for the Oxford and Cambridge Women's examinations, for the Royal Academy of Music and the Royal College of Music examinations, and for the Royal Society of Arts examinations, including painting and modelling' – modelling in 1906 meant moulding clay, not posing in front of a camera!

Dorothy did not board. Like most of her friends, she was a 'day-girl', walking the short distance from her Anlaby Road home. Father had introduced her to 'good' music from an early age, and now, under the guidance of Mrs. Russell-Starr, she learned to play the piano well, mastering the complications of harmony, playing in different keys, and learning to transpose with confidence. She practised daily on the walnut-fronted piano in the Denton's front parlour and soon became a confident performer. The school entered her for the Royal Academy of Music exams and she was presented with her certificate for the pianoforte at the Assembly Rooms in January 1908.

Julia Neilsen and Fred Terry in Hull, October 1906 at the Theatre Royal. Went with Father to see them on October 5th in 'Dorothy o' the Hall'.

The first of many references to theatre-going in Dorothy's diary. 'Pre-occupied with pleasure' was an accusation levelled at the Edwardians, but I wonder if it was fair comment. If they had spent even half their leisure hours at theatres, music halls and concerts, it would not have compared with the time we spend today watching television. It was an age when people had to go outside the home for their entertainment, with no radio, TV, or recorded music. Unless members of the family had the talent to play a musical instrument, and, of course, many had, the winter evenings would have to be spent sitting around the fire, reading, talking or playing games.

Small wonder that the theatres were packed with enthusiastic audiences. The Theatre Royal in Paragon Street was one of Hull's oldest, built and decorated in the extravagant style of the mid-Victorian age. It held just over a thousand and was considered 'elegantly small'. The interior of the theatre was maniloquent with pink and gold ornamentation, the proscenium decorated in floral gilt, and the stage curtains were a rich green velvet. The seats in the dress circle were comfortable fauteuils, upholstered in crimson with blue and gold stripes, whilst in the pit and stalls the audience sat on red velvet tip-up seats. The less affluent patrons in the gallery, or the 'gods', had to squeeze up tight on wooden forms. High above the auditorium hung a domed ceiling of eight decorated panels, with a powerful 'Sun-Burner' gas-light illuminating the auditorium.

Apart from the gallery seats at sixpence, which involved a long steep climb almost to the roof of the theatre, the cheapest seats were a shilling in the 'pit', at the back of the house. The side circle and stalls seats were three shillings, and the best seats in the centre-circle cost four shillings. Lady attendants walked up and down the aisles with trays of sweets and chocolates, but there were no ice-cream or fruit drinks on sale in the theatre in those days. Nor were there any cigarettes – a large notice advised patrons that, in the interests of safety, smoking was forbidden.

In the early days of its existence there had been some, mainly Methodists and factory owners, who had doubted the respectability of the Theatre Royal. But they could have found little to complain of in the performance of *Dorothy o' the Hall*, the story of the wooing of Dorothy Vernon of Haddon Hall. The critic of the *Hull Daily Mail* simpered:

'Most people who go to the theatre love sentimental moments. That is why they will love *Dorothy o' the Hall*. The story is steeped in sentiment. It radiates romance. How profound was the sigh which broke the silence at the Theatre Royal last night when Dorothy and her lover sealed their love in that first rapturous kiss. It was a sentimental moment if you will. What of Miss Julia Neilsen, the impersonator of Dorothy? In *Dorothy o' the Hall* we have Miss Neilsen at her best. So sweet a girl is Miss Neilsen that one gets quite a shock at seeing her lick her fingers after gnawing a chicken bone', an act which he suggested was an artistic mistake. Could such a breach of ladylike behaviour have been what the Mrs. Grundys had in mind when they doubted the theatre's respectability?

Dorothy o' the Hall had had an interesting history. When it had first been put on at the Gaiety Theatre in London in 1885 it had flopped. The Gaiety had a tradition of burlesque, but this kind of entertainment had little appeal to respectable married women; brazen, well-endowed females besported themselves on stage, while 'mashers' in the stalls trained their opera glasses on them. And the suggestive innuendo of the sketches shocked the matrons. In *Dorothy o' the Hall*, a sentimental light opera of 18th-century English country life, the management was convinced that they had a show which the respectable middle-classes would flock to see, just as they had for years patronised the wholesome Gilbert and Sullivan operas at the Savoy. But the regular Gaiety patrons were not keen on such a tame and sugary piece, and the press gave it poor notices. Even when it was transferred to the smaller Prince of Wales it languished and played to empty houses. It was not until new music was written and Marie Tempest introduced in the leading role that the play began to pick up. Eventually it ran for three years and made a fortune for its backers.

Went to the Trades Exhibition on October 17th 1906 with Father.

The six-week Trades Exhibition each autumn at the Artillery Barracks in Park Street became, for a few years, a regular event in Hull. It was put on to promote local trade, but for the majority of citizens it provided a

Jabez
(1862 - 1928)

Clara Ellen
(1864 - 1916)

Dorothy May
(1890 - 1968)

Charles Robert
(1892 - 1971)

Nellie
(1893 - 1965)

Edward Ernest
(1900 - 1975)

pleasant rendezvous where they could meet their friends and enjoy the music of the military bands. Dorothy loved it and went night after night. It was part of the new freedom that girls of Dorothy's generation were beginning to enjoy. It gave her the opportunity to mix freely with friends of both sexes. The exhibitions, and the new cinema age which was about to dawn, were a godsend to young people who sought a fleeting escape from the eye of Victorian parents.

The Trades Exhibition had become popular in Hull and other big cities after the Great International Exhibition in St. Louis in 1904 – the World Fair, immortalised years later by Judy Garland in the song *Meet Me in St. Louis*. The crowds flocked to Park Street, and the *Hull Daily Mail* commented that if the barracks had been twice as large it could have been filled.

Dorothy, of course, loved the music. A different band played each week: The Yorkshire Dragoons, the Blue Viennese, the Scots Guards, the Grenadier Guards, the Imperial Austrian and the Royal Marines. How splendid the bandsmen looked in their colourful uniforms, especially the handsome Viennese, playing all those lilting waltzes and stirring marches. They were enough to turn any girl's head.

The feature that caught everybody's eye that year was the prismatic fairy fountain. The *Hull Daily Mail* reporter described it enthusiastically: 'This remarkable fountain will be the talk of the Exhibition. A turn of the quick-acting lever and the spray is instantly regulated. 500 jets of various diameters will shoot forth 60,000 gallons of Corporation water twice daily. Overhead, from a platform suspended from the roof, four searchlights of 3,000 candle-power will illuminate through coloured screens the splashing water. The effects are beautiful. It is a veritable display of aqueous fireworks, the spray scattering like thousands of precious stones. There is refreshment to be enjoyed while listening to the band. In the courtyard around the bandstand, Cadburys have set out tables and chairs in Continental fashion. Here visitors will be able to sip their beverage, served by dainty waitresses in black dresses with white collars and cuffs. For a penny one gets a cup of cocoa and a biscuit, a sample of milk chocolate, and a small tin of cocoa. Busy people are in the habit of saying, 'I've no time for anything – not even meals!' They should take Oxo for it is just the quick-time meal required. It contains the stimulating and nourishing properties of finest beef, and is the quick meal of health for strenuous people. Athletes find Oxo invaluable. C.B. Fry uses it when cup-tie training.'

Not least of the attractions at the Exhibition were the free samples of merchandise offered by the exhibitors. Visitors could take home carrier-bags filled with miniature jars of jam and marmalade, meat paste, biscuits, cocoa, custard powder, jelly, toffees and sweets, toothpaste, shoe polish, to say nothing of booklets, pamphlets, puzzles and games.

Many of the innovations of the age were there to be examined and tried out. Housewives were reported to marvel at the glittering row of stoves displayed in the Gas Room for their approval, and the latest labour-saving device, the Air Suction Cleaning Machine, the fore-runner of the Hoover, was on show, although the lady of the house needed to have muscles like a blacksmith to push the heavy machine around the house.

The younger visitors were apparently very much like the teenagers of today, and liked their music played at ear-splitting volume; they were catered for on a stand displaying Edison, Zonophone or Sterling phonographs, fitted with variegated flower horns, which were said to improve the tone. The gold-plated, de-luxe model at £35 could, the makers claimed, be heard three miles away.

Cravens, the jam-makers displayed their products with flair. Jars of their Seville orange marmalade were set out with the latest electric lamps behind them, 'so that the brilliance of electric light shines through them and produces the effect of golden sunshine'.

The crowds marvelled at the progress of the age. The Exhibition provided all the fun of the fair, without its vulgarity. And, no doubt, Dorothy found opportunities to escape from Father's watchful eye.

Nellie's birthday November 5th. Father took us all to fireworks and bonfire in West Park.

Life in the Denton household centred around Father, the head of the household. Jabez Denton was a neat and tidy little man who dressed formally, always with a fresh flower in his buttonhole, and his grey moustache was stiffly waxed to a sharp point at each end. His children addressed him as 'Father' and showed him considerable respect, as did his wife, Clara. Patriarchal authority was an essential part of the fabric of Edwardian family life, and Jabez commanded respect; his very name, stern and Biblical, discouraged the kind of familiarities that might have been taken with a Tom, Dick or Harry.

Jabez was the head cashier of the Yorkshire Insurance Company, which he had joined as a boy of 16, and which he was to serve all his working life. His respectable employment earned for the Denton family a comfortable middle-class status. Grandfather, Samuel Denton, had left his village of Hotham in 1820 and set himself up in Bond Street as a butcher, a trade in which his son Charles had succeeded him, and in which he had made a good living. Unencumbered by a large family, for fortune – but for Hannah Denton's untimely death he might have been the eldest of a large family and not enjoyed the advantages of a good his wife, Hannah, had died giving birth to Jabez, he had educated and lavished care on his only child.

In 1885 Jabez married Clara Helen Dobson, the second of three daughters of Robert Dobson, a Bridlington saddler. Seven years after their marriage, and shortly after the birth of their first child, Dorothy, they had bought a villa in Newington, which was then on the outskirts of the town. They named it Oban Villa, after the Scottish resort where they had spent their honeymoon. It was directly opposite the gates of West Park, and in this pleasantly situated house they brought up their family of two girls and two boys. Dorothy always said her parents might well have had a dozen children but for Clara's frequent miscarriages during the early days of their marriage.

If Jabez appeared to be the archetypal Victorian father, that is not to imply that he was an overbearing man – he was, in fact, a man of good humour, even tempered and with a wide range of interests. The unvarying routine of his work had developed in him a man of regular habits. Punctually at 8.30 each morning he would board the 'A' tram-car, which stopped almost at his front door, and travel into town, taking a seat upstairs so that he could smoke his pipe and read his *Eastern Morning News*. Alighting at Monument Bridge, he walked the short distance down Whitefriargate to his Lowgate office where he presided over the Yorkshire Insurance Co. accounts from 9 am to 5.30 pm. He lunched each day at Miss Thompson's cafe where, Dorothy always maintained, the waitress never gave him a bill, trusting him to settle with Miss Thompson at the end of the week. As permanent a fixture in the office as the oak desk and the leather-bound ledgers, Jabez enjoyed the full confidence of Mr. Heslewood, the Resident Secretary, and he in his turn, held E.E.H. in such respect that he named his second son Ernest Edward after him. Office protocol was strict, and the staff always addressed him as Mr. Denton; the juniors called him 'sir'. The use of first names in the office would have been unthinkable in 1900, and only among his friends at the Hull Bowling Club, or his fellow sidesmen at St. Matthew's in the Boulevard, was he known as 'Denny'.

Fading family photographs show how formally the Edwardian office worker dressed – even on the beach at Filey Jabez clung to his dark suit with high stiff collar, and seldom ventured forth without his waistcoat, from the pockets of which hung a heavy gold watch chain; on his head a dignified grey Homberg hat, and on his feet a pair of well polished boots. If we could have seen him at the table we should have noted that he was always served before the rest of the family, and the bottle of Lee and Perrin's sauce set before him was exclusively for his use. If his privileges strike us as old-fashioned and autocratic, they were considered then as no more than his due. Jabez, I think, recognised his good education and financial security. He had a fund of sayings, and one of his favourites was, 'We know now what we are, but we know not what we may be' – he might well have added, 'or what we might have been'. Jabez and Clara Denton were born and grew up in Victorian times, and the changes which had taken place in the first years of the new century must, to them, have seemed overwhelming. The start of Edward VII's reign had brought restless times, with the first flimsy aeroplane whirring across the sky, noisy, dirty motor cars kicking up clouds of dust, the clamour of militant women for the vote, the clatter of typewriters and the intrusion of telephones into the office, and new-fangled gas cookers replacing the old kitchen range in the house. The upheaval of society, which war was to accelerate in a few years time, had begun. But these changes were as nothing to those Dorothy was to see before she died.

Teddie commenced with measles on Friday 7th December, 1906.

Poor Teddie, Dorothy's six-year old brother, was not the most robust of lads. Due to his delicate health he had not yet started school. Now he had measles just before Christmas. The doctor would, of course, have instructed Clara on the care of the patient: he must be kept warm in bed, with the curtains tightly closed – not a chink of light was to be allowed to penetrate the room, otherwise the effect on the boy's eyesight could be most serious. He would have to remain in this state for at least a fortnight, but with proper care he might just be well enough to come downstairs for Christmas dinner.

Medical practice at the time still harboured some very odd notions. There were doctors who believed that appendicitis was a contagious disease; diabetes was incurable, as was tuberculosis, and millions still died of the wasting consumption; rickets deformed the limbs of countless numbers of children of the poor. Good food and housing enabled the better-off to escape many of these debilitating illnesses, and Jabez was in the fortunate position of being able to ensure that his own children grew up healthy. Even Teddie overcame his childhood ailments and lived to enjoy his full three-score-and-ten years, and a few more as well!

The newspapers of the day were full of advertisements for patent medicines. Many of the claims were extravagant, to say the least, if not downright fraudulent. An advert like the following would surely have fallen foul of the Trades Description Act, if such had existed in 1906:

A SCHOOLGIRL, A VICTIM OF ST. VITUS' DANCE, SPEECHLESS AND PARALYSED, NOW A BRIGHT, ROSY, HEALTHY GIRL, CURED BY DR. WILLIAMS' PINK PILLS.

Nellie and I went to Bridlington on Tuesday 11th December and stayed at Grandma's. Went to a Pleasant Saturday Evening on Dec. 15th. Went to a lecture on Japan at Wesley Schoolroom. Came home from Brid on December 24th.

Clara had her hands full with Teddie ill in bed, and packed her two daughters off to Grandma's – perhaps neither of the girls had had measles, and she did not want three children sick at Christmas. Nellie was Dorothy's younger sister, then an attractive 13-year old, clever, lively, and a very popular girl at the Boulevard Higher Grade, where she promised to be a gifted pupil.

Jabez took the girls down to Paragon Station and saw them onto the Bridlington train, and Aunt Kate, Clara's elder sister, met them in. Mr. Anson's ancient cab conveyed them and their luggage to Grandma Dobson's house in Tennyson Avenue. The old lady had already put the stone hot water bottles in the big feather bed for the girls. Theirs was a warm and cosy bedroom which I remember from my own childhood; at the foot of the bed hung two pictures, one of an impudent boy holding out a rosy apple, and teasing the girl in the other picture: 'Would you like a bite?', she shyly replying, 'I know you don't mean it!'

The Denton children looked forward to holidays at Bridlington. I don't think Clara took well to life in the city, and looked on her girlhood home in Bridlington as a refuge from the humdrum routine of life at 409 Anlaby Road. At any rate, she and the children seldom missed an opportunity of spending the school holidays at Bridlington. Grandma's house was roomy with six bedrooms (if you counted the attics), and was full of solid Victorian furniture. On the passage wall were glass cases of stuffed animals and birds, trophies which had once graced Grandpa's saddlery shop in King Street. Neither of the girls remembered him for he had died shortly after Dorothy was born, but his presence could still be felt in the house: in one of the attics Grandma kept the tools he had used as a saddler and harness-maker, along with fishing rods and other sporting gear he had once sold in his shop.

Kate, Grandma Dobson's eldest daughter, had never married. She was now well into her forties and had long resigned herself to spinsterhood. The only man she had ever considered marrying had gone out to Australia in the 1890s and had wanted to take her with him. Whether it was the ties of home, and the reluctance to leave a widowed mother, or the uncertainty of life in an untamed land 14,000 miles from home that deterred Kate from marriage, I do not know. There was, too, a dark secret in the Dobson family which she would have had to disclose if she had married: that her baptised name was Kate Ainsworth, and not Kate Dobson. Both she and her elder brother, Fred, had been born to Anna Ainsworth before Robert Dobson married her. Even though he made an honest woman of her before Dorothy's mother and the other sister were born, her parents' indiscretion had stigmatised poor Kate for life. It may well have been the reason why brother Fred left home at an early age and Kate remained single. Having no children of her own, Kate was a devoted aunt to her nephews and nieces, and, in later years, to their children too.

She had taken the girls to the Wesley Schoolroom for the lecture on Japan, a country about which the West knew very little in those days. Hull, however, had a special interest in this distant land, for Japan and Russia had recently been at war. In 1904 the Czar's warships had mistaken Hull trawlers fishing off the Dogger Bank for a Japanese naval force and had opened fire, sinking several ships and killing fishermen. The people of Hull had, of course, been on the side of the Japanese, but they could have little guessed how treacherously the Japanese would treat their former friends 40 years later.

'Votes for Women' - a lively issue when Dorothy was young.

Dorothy Denton.

1907

Tuesday 8th January 1907. Went to Doris and Jack's Whist Drive. Won first prize, a silver buttonhook.

Doris and Jack Fenner were cousins of the Dentons. Clara Denton's younger sister, Jane Anne, known as Jinnie, had married Harry Fenner in 1887. He was quite a catch, the joint managing director, with brother Walter, of the firm of J.H. Fenner, a company their father had established some years before for the manufacture of leather machine belting. The Fenners had seven children. In 1907 Elsie, the eldest, was 19; her younger sister, Gertie, a very pretty girl, was Dorothy's age and her confidante, whilst Doris and brother Jack were a year or two younger. The Fenners lived near the Dentons at 379, Anlaby Road.

Whist drives were the social craze of the day: people ran whist drives in their homes as a means of entertaining their friends and raising small amounts for charity. It would be difficult to imagine whist drives having any appeal for today's teenagers, but these events were immensely popular in Edwardian times, even among the young. Public whist drives were held in church halls for many years, and were as well supported in their day as their successors, the Saturday-night hop and Bingo.

The *Hull Daily Mail*, writing about church-hall whist drives, described them as 'an outlet for the social sympathies of middle-class girls', but it warned that 'a young woman who arrives at maturity with no deeper experience of social ameneties than can be gathered at such functions, will be wanting in the lighter graces'. And there were other pitfalls to beware of by mixing too freely at such functions with people who might afterwards be 'apt to presume'. How awful for a well-brought-up young lady to be stopped in the street by some plebeian person with whom she had played cards the previous week, 'presuming' to engage her in conversation

But the Fenners' whist drive was a private one, so Dorothy would have been among friends. And she won the first prize, a silver buttonhook. Buttonhooks were used in the days before zip-fasteners, when the fashionable boots which young ladies wore were secured around the calf by a dozen or more small buttons, the fastening of which was nearly impossible without the aid of a buttonhook. Dressing and undressing for the Edwardian girl was a good deal more complicated than it is today for her great-grand-daughter. In winter a young girl of Dorothy's generation would first have put on a thick woollen vest, followed by her stays. These were made of a sort of linen and usually had ten buttons down the front; around the waist-line of these stays were a number of linen buttons, on to which she fastened her drawers, and these came down to an inch below her knees. She would then put on her flanelette petticoat, over which she would drape a second one of red flannel, buttonholed and embroidered around the hem. Her winter dress was most likely of warm merino wool, and she wore black woollen stockings and button-boots. She had to be well insulated against the chill of Edwardian homes without the benefit of central heating. In the street she would wear a coat, or pelisse, a sort of double cape, with wool hat and gloves to keep out the cold January wind.

For social occasions, such as the Fenner whist drive, Dorothy would have worn a high-necked dress or a bodice with the long trailing skirt of the day. Most women fastened a strip of brush-braid around the hem to ward off the dirt of the pavements. Girls obviously took trouble to look their best at whist drives where boys would be present; a newspaper of the day commented that 'but for whist drives, many girls who have little opportunity of meeting the opposite sex would remain spinsters'.

Went to see 'Amasis' at the Grand Theatre with Gertie and Ma on 28th February 1907. Constance Drewer, Rutland Barrington and Roland Cunningham, principals.

According to the programme, this comic-opera was the story of an Egyptian princess at the court of the Pharaoh at Memphis. These ancient Egyptians had such reverence for the ibis, the crocodile, and the cat that, at a time of extreme famine, they ate one another rather than feed on their imagined deities. Cannibalism does not sound a very attractive theme, but *Amasis* was a spectacular show with a large cast and exotic settings. It was sufficiently well received in Hull for it to be booked for a return visit to the Grand later in the year – rather like the 'repeats' which we complain so much about on our television today

The Grand Opera House was Hull's leading theatre and staged the big West End shows when they came on their provincial tour . It was an imposing building on the north side of George Street, later to be converted into the Dorchester cinema, with a stone portico and a wide balcony across its front. On summer evenings the gentlemen in the audience could step out on to this balcony and enjoy a smoke during the interval. Double mahogany doors at the front of the theatre gave access to a fine vestibule decorated in gold and other rich colours, and the audience then ascended a wide marble staircase, divided by double bold

Theatre Royal,
Paragon Street,
Hull;
later replaced
by the Tivoli.

Lowgate, Hull.
The hansom cab is
passing the
Yorkshire
Insurance offices,
where Jabez Denton
was head cashier.

brass handrails into the principal lounge. It was the custom for the social hob-nobbers to linger here, chatting to friends and acquaintances, until the theatre bell summoned them to their seats.

The lounge, according to contemporary reports, was beautifully decorated with carved balusters, rails and arched entrances draped with rich terra-cotta draperies. The doors, windows and fittings were finished in white porcelain picked out in gold, the walls decorated with blue and gold Japanese paper, and the ceiling richly decorated. The auditorium was equally impressive. Private boxes flanked the stage, each draped with stamped-gold plush curtains and valance, trimmed with heliotrope silk. The richly decorated ceiling was divided by scroll-work pilasters, and the panels adorned with winged cupids; at each corner were paintings representing Art, Painting, Music and Singing. The gallery and dress circle fronts were decorated in gold, and had peacocks with brass collars carrying small electric lamps.

Tastes in decorative art have changed a lot since Dorothy's day, but the Edwardian theatre was splendid by comparison with the drab homes in which most members of the audience lived, and the luxury of being in such opulent surroundings for an hour or two was as much a part of the evening out as the show itself.

Went with Father to see 'Peter Pan' on April 10th, 1907. Zena Dare as Peter, Ella Q. May as Wendy.

Zena Dare was one of the darlings of the Edwardian stage. When she came to play at the Grand Theatre in Hull in 1907 in J.M. Barrie's new play, *Peter Pan*, she was not yet 20-years-old and already a big star. Mass idolisation of popular entertainers had not yet become the vogue, but stars like Zena Dare and her younger sister, Phyllis, enjoyed a mass following. Although details of their private lives were not made public in newspapers and fan magazines, there was a craze for collecting picture postcards of the stars. Thousands of pictures of the Dare sisters in their different costumes were sold to the public, and the stars received endless letters asking for these postcards to be signed. One of the first matinée idols of the day to attract his own 'fan club' was Lewis Waller, who was so popular with his female fans that they started the K.O.W., (Keen on Waller) club in his honour.

This was the era of the 'Stage-door Johnnies', the fashionable young men (and some not so young), who hung around the stage-doors of the West End theatres for the privilege of taking one of these glamorous ladies out for supper. Outside the Gaiety and Daly's and His Majesty's theatres could be seen long lines of hansom cabs waiting at the stage-door to take them off to the Savoy or the Carlton Grill, and huge bouquets of flowers were delivered to the dressing rooms. And not only flowers, for often a present would be hung in the bouquet, and one had to look carefully in case a trinket got lost. Sometimes they were valuable diamond brooches or bracelets, and then a decision had to be made whether to return them to the sender. Nice girls didn't keep expensive jewels.

In the tradition of the Edwardian stage Zena Dare married into the aristocracy, but it was not quite a 'rags-to-riches' story; she was the daughter of a country solicitor and a musical mother who had wished to become an actress. On the night in 1904 when she had first won acclaim in *The Catch of the Season*, two of the many admirers who called backstage to congratulate her had been Lord Esher and his younger son, the Hon. Maurice Brett, an officer in the Guards. They stood there, father and son, two gentlemen in top hats and opera cloaks with their golden-knobbed canes, lost in admiration of the young star. Maurice made up his mind there and then: he was determined to marry her, and, even though it took him another six years, he managed to persuade her. But in those days a Guards officer who married an actress had to resign his commission, however respectable she might be, and Captain Brett had to quit the Brigade of Guards. Lucky for him, many may have thought. His regiment was wiped out almost to a man at the beginning of the war.

Dorothy was an ardent admirer of the Dare sisters and noted both their birthdays at the back of her diary, along with their correct family name, but whether she was fan enough to write to them I cannot say.

Went to Bridlington on Tuesday April 22nd 1907 and stayed a week and a day. While there went with Auntie for a day to Speeton and gathered primroses on the cliffs.

Dorothy and Aunt Kate took the train to Speeton in 1907, but later that year they might have driven there by motor bus. The *Bridlington Free Press* announced the coming of the newest form of transport: 'All who have pitied the distressed horses late on a summer's night, yoked to the buses plying between the Quay and the Old Town, will be glad to hear that, through the enterprise of Mr. John Williamson, a Bridlington motor bus will shortly be running. Yesterday a trial trip, previous to the issuing of a licence, was made. The Town Council was represented by its most 'weighty' members, including the Mayor, Councillor Mainprize, the Deputy Mayor, and a full body of councillors. The Town Clerk, the Borough Engineer, and the Carriage Inspector were also present. The motor bus drew out of Mr. Williamson's premises on Quay Road and halted at the end of Brett Street, where a photograph was taken by Mr. Gibson of the bus and its passengers.

'A start was then made, and proceeding by way of St. John Street, High Street, Market Place and the Scarborough Road, the bus toiled up to the Dotterel Inn, where a stop was made for refreshments.'

'The passengers having been regaled, they again mounted the bus, and it was driven to Speeton, stayed there while some legal business was transacted by officers of the Council, after which a smart run to Bridlington was made by way of Bempton, Flamborough Station and Sewerby. The bus, which will seat 38 passengers, has been supplied by Mr. Hoyle of Brighouse.'

It was one of those bright, early Spring days when Dorothy and Aunt Kate walked from the station at Speeton, along windswept lanes to the cliff top. The sun shone, and the brisk sea breeze flattened their long skirts against their legs as they held on with both hands to their hats. On the cliff edge, where the stunted trees leaned with the prevailing wind, a flock of curlews alighted among the tufted grasses, and high above, and almost out of sight, the skylarks were in full Spring voice. The view from Speeton cliffs in the sharp sunlit air was reward enough for the struggle against the wind. In one direction they looked to the high white cliffs of Bempton, where thousands of nesting seabirds wheeled and screeched in the wind. To the North, over the wide sweep of Primrose Valley and Filey Bay, the rugged outcrop of the Yorkshire Wolds tumbled into the sea, forming a rocky promontory over which a restless sea broke in white spray. A dangerous stretch of coast, and Aunt Kate used to recite the sailors' warning:

> 'Flamborough Head as we sail by,
> Filey Brig we daren't go nigh;
> Scarborough Castle stands out to sea,
> And Whitby rocks lie Northerly.'

And the primroses that Dorothy picked on Speeton cliffs, so soon to fade and wither in her hands – was she remembering them years later when she wrote:

> 'Flowers are the brightest things,
> That earth on her broad bosom loves to cherish;
> Gay they appear as children's mirth,
> Like fading dreams of hope they perish.'

Went with Mrs. Lambert on Thursday 13th June 1907 round Reckitt's Blue and Starch Works. Saw blue, starch, black-lead etc. made, boxes and tins.

I should think this educational visit that Dorothy made with Aston High School was one of the few occasions when she saw inside a factory. Reckitt's were Hull's biggest manufacturer, known world-wide for their *Robin Starch* and *Reckitt's Blue*, washday staples that the housewife relied on before washing machines and detergents took most of the drudgery out of Monday mornings. They were famed for their *Brasso* metal polish, and that bane of the housemaid's life, *Lion Black Lead* and *Zebra Grate Polish*, a carbonaceous paste which she had to spread on the kitchen range and fireplace – both filthy and detested jobs.

How, I wonder, did Reckitt's factory girls react to a group of well-dressed young women, with soft hands and manicured nails, being conducted around the factory floor? I can imagine the comments they muttered to each other: 'Stuck-up, toffee-nosed lot! What do they want 'ere?' The middle classes held themselves consciously aloof from the working class, who for their part resented their superior airs. The middle-class sounded their aitches and spoke grammatically, they observed the correct ritual at table (how one held one's knife and fork was a sure give-away), and cultivated a taste for music, art, and literature. Above all, they abhorred the moral turpitude of the working-class with their improvidence and indulgence in drink. The working man was seen by his 'betters' as a 'loud-voiced, independent, arrogant figure, with a thirst for drink, imperfect standards of decency, and a determination to be supported at somebody else's expense'. *The Times* declared of the lower orders: 'their wages would suffice to keep them strong and healthy, but they are thriftless: they drink or bet, or are ignorant and careless in housekeeping'.

But poverty in Hull and in every other big city was very real. Nobody could shut their eyes to the appalling conditions in which numbers of poor people lived. 'Mother Humber' had written during the winter in her column in the *Hull Daily Mail*:

'At poverty's gate are we still, I am sorry to say, with hundreds of cases of near starvation – men, women and children living in homes entirely devoid of any furniture, and, in some instances, where there has been no fire for days, or any food but what scraps sympathetic neighbours have given to keep them alive.'

But then 'Mother Humber' went on to complain that the Poor Rate in Sculcoates had risen to 4/8d in the £, and there were more paupers than ever dependent on the workhouse: 'Of course, I don't mean to say that the workhouse inmate is too lavishly or luxuriously treated, although I do feel that many aged or sick people have comforts in the workhouse that they could not have in their own homes...one cannot but feel that all extravagances ought to be looked at by our Guardians.'

An all too common sight in Hull on freezing cold days were the barefoot children who begged in the streets, and 'John Humber' had commented:

'I hope something will be done for the starving urchins who loiter about Paragon Station and our leading streets. Their presence is nothing short of scandalous. It is not a new complaint. I have made it before. It has been under official notice at the Town Hall, but nothing is done, and in the bitter weather we have had lately the nuisance has been worse than before. If the police do not act, some of our societies can take the matter up. It is sheer cruelty to the children. If the case of the parents is found on enquiry to be a deserving one, they can be relieved. But it is absolutely indefensible to allow such cruelty to be practised in our public streets for the purpose of squeezing coppers from the charitable.'

They were hard times, and many people had hard hearts to match.

Admiral Charles Beresford passed our house in a motor car on Saturday June 29th, 1907.

Motor cars were still sufficiently rare for Dorothy to comment on the Admiral of the Channel Fleet passing their house in this novel form of transport. Cars were as yet the plaything of the rich, although here and there a forward-looking doctor had bought one to drive around to visit his patients. It was only a matter of a year or two since the law limiting these 'horseless carriages' to four miles an hour, and requiring a man to walk in front with a red flag, had been repealed. By 1907 they had become rather more acceptable, and the speed limit had been raised to 20 m.p.h., but there was still prejudice in some quarters against these noisy, stinking contraptions. A recent case reported in the *Hull Daily Mail:*

'A chauffeur named James Adams was a defendant at Hull Police Court today for driving a motor car at a dangerous speed. Pc. Lamb said he saw Adams driving a motor car along Alfred Gelder Street towards Monument Bridge at a high speed which he estimated at 12 miles an hour. As the car came opposite Peterson's fish shop it swerved in front of a tram car causing it to slow down. The defendant claimed that 12 m.p.h. was the maximum speed of which the car was capable, and he was only on the second gear. The Bench found the case proved and fined the defendant 40 shillings and ordered him to pay the solicitor's fee . . .'

Whitefriargate, once Hull's busiest shopping street.

Girls stripping Zebra Paste polish tins at Reckitt's.

Admiral Lord Charles Beresford was a popular hero of the day, an aristocratic figure and a personal friend of the King, and he, like his Sovereign, was reputed to have an eye for the ladies. In the years leading up to the outbreak of War the Royal Navy was held in high esteem as Britain's shield against the vaunting ambitions of the German Kaiser. The Navy at the time was being strengthened by the building of six formidable *Dreadnoughts*. But the patrician Lord Charles Beresford was in conflict over these ships with his Commander-in-Chief, Lord Fisher, a man of humbler birth, and their disagreements were widely reported in the press. A Court scandal, however, proved to be Lord Charles Beresford's ultimate undoing. He was unwise enough to quarrel with the King over a lady who shared her favours with both of them, and was reputed to have threatened His Majesty, and to have shaken his fist under the royal nose.

But in 1907 it was esteemed a great honour that the Admiral was bringing his fleet to visit the Humber ports, and the local councils vied with each other to provide hospitality and entertainment for our gallant sailors. £100 was voted by Cleethorpes Entertainment Committee for the entertainment of 800 men, a hundred from each ship. Councillor Brockwood, Chairman of the Committee, was reported as saying that 'this would provide each man with a good dinner and a gift of tobacco, and there would be sports on the sands, such as donkey-racing and a tug-of-war between the ships, the worthy councillor added: 'This will be good publicity for the town, and we are only doing our duty as patriotic Englishmen in entertaining the Navy'. He unctuously added, 'Admiral Lord Charles Beresford, being such a splendid Englishman, would take it as a personal compliment to himself . . .'

Sad to relate, the draught of water in the Humber that weekend turned out to be too low for the Admiral to bring his ships up the river to Hull, so the citizens had to be satisfied with the sight of the great man in the back of a motor car, and not on the quarter-deck of his flag-ship.

Received an autograph album from Tom on Wednesday 10th July, 1907.

When a young person in Edwardian days asked a friend to write something in his or her album it offered great scope for the artist, poet, or wit to pay a charming compliment to its owner. The invitation to 'put something in my book' was seldom declined. The autograph book which Tommy Andrews gave to Dorothy in 1907 became a cherished possession, preserved in her lifetime and passed down to her descendants, a relic of an age when people had the time to express themselves in thoughtful and creative ways..

On the first page, pink and yellow roses, painted in pale water colours, were Tommy's own personal bouquet, a token of his affection for the girl of 17 he was 'sweet on'. And roses too expressed the sentiments of the man Dorothy was to marry, who wrote in 1920 in his stylish hand, 'We find a thorn with every rose, but ain't the roses sweet' – poor Cyril, who was to suffer life's thorns in the years ahead.

The pages of Dorothy's album still trace the memories of her youth, the fading water-colours, the artistic pen-and-ink sketches, the dated Edwardian humour, the romantic verses, the original and the oft-quoted sayings of 80 years ago. On one page Ken Hutchinson, a New Zealand cousin serving in England during the First War with the ANZAC forces, invited her (in green ink), to 'Come and have tea with me at the Kardomah Cafe' (in Whitefriargate if I remember rightly). A Canadian soldier, with rare artistic skill, painted the feathered head of an American Indian, and wistfully wrote, 'I stand in a land of roses, but I dream of a land of snow.' Lines from Goethe, and stodgy Germanic poetry in the old German script, which today nobody can read, were written by Dorothy's pre-war German friends.

The hands that filled those pages have long been still – some of the young men did not live to see middle age, and each page held for Dorothy a memory of friends who passed in and out of her life in those far-off days before the Great War.

Went to Bridlington for the day on July 31st '07. Spent morning and afternoon on the Parade and at night went on Spa to see Professor Gaudion go up in a balloon. Came down into the sea by parachute.

Flying was still something of a sensation in the summer of 1907, and Dorothy and her friends would certainly not yet have seen a 'flying machine'. Bleriot's historic flight over the Channel was still two years away. But air balloons were already familiar, and daring young men like 'Professor' Gaudion entertained holiday crowds by ascending to several hundred feet in a balloon over the sea, leaping out of the basket, and descending gently on a parachute to where a launch was waiting to pick them up.

The previous year a certain Alfred von Mans and his companion, Lieutenant Cranatti, had created a stir in the sleepy village of New Holland, across the river from Hull, by making a sensational descent in their balloon on to the roofs of some cottages, tearing off chimney pots and damaging tiles and windows. The intrepid birdmen, who had been blown off course during a race from Paris to London, were, according to the *Hull Daily Mail*, rescued by ladder, and as soon as they reached the safety of the ground both men, by now black from head to foot with the soot of the broken chimneys, kissed each other heartily.

Went to Bridlington for the last fortnight in August, and to Filey for the first fortnight in Sept. '07. While in Filey went to Scarborough for a day with Father and Gertie on Friday 13th. Went on Filey Brig. Stayed at Granby House, Rutland Street.

A month by the sea – how fortunate the family who could escape from the city at the height of summer for 28 whole days. Bridlington had grown in the early years of the century into a popular seaside resort for the North of England, but for most people the annual holiday was a week, or at best a fortnight, in a boarding house. Holidays with pay were still a far-off dream. Even the lucky ones who managed to get away had to watch the pennies, and the burden of looking after the family still fell on mother. She shopped as she had at home, but left the cooking to the landlady, who would charge her guests 21/- a week for 'room and attendance', or perhaps 25/- if she offered a bathroom instead of the usual jug and basin on a marble-topped stand.

Bridlington in 1907 was very different in character from what it has become today. Before the popularity of seaside holidays for the working masses, which came about after the Great War, there was an air of quiet refinement about the place. Visitors strolled the Esplanade, listened to the bands on the Royal Princes Parade, and were entertained by concert parties at the Spa Hall. The holidaymakers of those days were always respectably dressed – even those who ventured on to the beach would not have dreamed of discarding their city clothes, not even of going hatless. They sat on the sands, some of them in deckchairs, wearing the same clothing as they wore at home – the men in high stiff collars and ties, with their dark worsted suits, bowler hats, and boots, while the women suffered uncomplainingly on summer days in long-sleeved blouses and trailing skirts. Even the children, constricted in their thick hot clothes, thought it a great treat to be allowed to take off their shoes and stockings and paddle in the sea.

The poorer people had to be content with a day-trip to the seaside. Hornsea and Withernsea, being much nearer to Hull, attracted most of the day-trippers, but Brid had its share. The better-off hated them, and some of the snobbier resorts in the South banned Sunday trains to keep them away; no music or entertainment was allowed on the Parade or on the Spa, and none of the amusements were open on Sundays. The day-trippers flocked to the beaches, but Jabez Denton, a man of convention, would never have allowed his family to take such liberties with the Sabbath.

A report in the Hull Daily Mail on August Bank Holiday in 1907 describes the summer exodus:

'Probably never in Bridlington's history has the rush to the town been so great as in the 48 hours ending on Saturday night. One train-load of visitors at noon chartered every one of the cavalcade of conveyances that ply within the purlieus of the railway station, and wanted more. Then they adapted themselves to the circumstances; men climbed on to the roof of the omnibuses and, snug among the holiday baggage, were whirled away to their temporary homes.'

'The tension placed upon the railway staff was almost intolerable. Hour by hour the mountains of 'luggage-in-advance' piled higher and higher, thousands of pieces being handled and delivered between Thursday and Saturday. All roads led to Bridlington, and a railway carriage that did not contain a complement of sixteen was not half-filled. Never was a holiday so richly earned as in the getting there. It was, though, a good humoured rush.'

On the following day it was reported that, 'Brilliant sunshine favoured the thousands of holiday-makers on Monday, and the whole multifarious sources of attractions were absolutely besieged. The wind had lost its power and sting of the previous day and left the day peacefully calm. With the tide at the flood, a charming spectacle was presented. The entire fleet of cobles, small pleasure boats and skiffs which Bridlington possesses, were dotted all over the wide sweep of the bay, with important little motor launches dashing in and out of the harbour on their excursions to the Head. The portion of the beach reserved for mixed bathing seems to have been an irresistible attraction for the multitude. The crowd here was densest, enjoying the humorous incidents – gay cavaliers instructing timid ladies in the natatorial art. The whole aquatic scene was both novel and interesting.'

The day had not, however, been without its drama. Again quoting the *Hull Daily Mail*:

'A magistrate's court on Thursday had a ladies' bathing costume of full size produced to them in court, and they were asked to give an opinion as to whether a lady bathing in such a costume appeared improperly clad. The gentleman who made this somewhat startling request was Major Pinkhurst, a visitor who was charged with having assaulted another visitor, namely Henry Grant.

Music on the sea front at Bridlington, 1907.

Holiday crowds watching the Pierrots on the North Sands, Bridlington.

Mr. Grant said he was sitting on the beach with his three ladies. The major's wife and daughter had been bathing. On emerging from the water the major's wife accused him of making insulting remarks about her appearance. The major came up and struck him in the face. He denied that he had made any offensive remarks.

The major said he pleaded guilty to the charge absolutely and without the slightest hesitation. He heard Grant remark that his (the major's) wife was disreputable in her bathing costume, and anyone who heard such remarks from a total stranger would do exactly as he did – strike him. Grant was gazing at his wife and waiting for her to come out of the water. 'I lost my temper,' added the major, 'and struck him, as I would strike any man saying so insulting things about my wife. I should not be a man if I didn't. He was such a cur that he bolted, would not face me, strike me, or return the blow.' Major Pinkhurst, on being ordered to pay a penalty of 19/6d, remarked that it was worth three or four sovereigns to knock such a man about.'

The early September fortnight in Filey was a perennial favourite with the Dentons, and Jabez always booked his annual holiday to coincide with the Scarborough Cricket Festival. It was one of the few opportunities he had each summer to watch his County, then at the peak of their sporting power. As a Yorkshire member, Jabez did not get a lot of cricket for his subscription, for the County only played one first-class match each season in Hull, and that year the Hull members had had particularly poor value; the scheduled three-day match with Leicestershire had been all but over after the first day. There had been rain in Hull earlier in the week, and on the Wednesday Yorkshire had caught their opponents on a 'sticky wicket'. Pitches were left uncovered in those days and the hot sun had dried out the wet pitch, making George Hirst almost unplayable. Leicestershire were dismissed for 60, and in reply Yorkshire could manage only 114, but the visitors had succumbed for only 54 in their second innings, leaving Yorkshire to score but one run for a ten-wickets win. Hirst took 15 wickets for 63, but left the local members bemoaning the loss of almost two days'   cricket from their meagre allocation.

Hilda married October 9th, 1907

Hilda had been the Denton's housemaid for two years and took her leave of them when she married. In 1907 domestic service provided employment for nearly a million English women. Every day there were lengthy columns of 'Help Wanted' in the local newspapers for cooks, housemaids, parlourmaids, and for the ubiquitous 'general'. The pay offered was minimal – around £20 a year for an experienced cook, a housemaid/parlourmaid £16 to £18, and the wage for a 'general' varied according to age, from £14 at age 23 to £10 at 19, the wage, of course, including food and accommodation.

Sometimes employers specified the duties required – cleaning silver, plain sewing, waiting at table *etc.* – but the duties were as varied as they were limitless. On the other hand, servants too could be choosy. Size of family was important, for few women wanted to be the drudge of a large family, and where other help was employed this was stated, or implied, as in 'no washing', and in, the case of one lady who advertised that she had gas-fires, the presumption was that a prospective employee would not have to perform the tiresome chore of laying fires and cleaning grates. The hours were long and the work hard, but while one employer promised 'liberal outings', another stipulated that an applicant 'must be an early riser'. Age limits varied – 40 was about the upper limit – and, at the other end, a post offered for a 14-year old girl was described as 'a wonderful opportunity'. All employers demanded women of good character (one stipulated 'Church of England only'), and satisfactory references were, of course, essential.

Clara Denton was not a difficult mistress to work for: she was not the kind of employer who followed her servants around the house, running her hands over surfaces to check that they had been dusted. But she had been very angry once with a girl who had knocked over and broken some cherished porcelain figures; she swore the girl had done it for spite and sacked her without a reference. For all the cheapness of domestic labour, the complaints of the middle classes about the shortcomings of their servants were endless:

'John Humber's' column in the *Hull Daily Mail* under the heading 'UPSETTING THE HOUSEHOLD' reported: 'I have heard girls say that their mistress did not treat them well. Does the average servant girl treat her mistress very well? Why, she begins in the morning by not getting up on time, serving the breakfast late, and starting the husband off to work without a decent breakfast, the wife sore at heart, troubled.

'A girl going into a factory soon learns obedience. She has to obey the forewoman at once, and without question, and she soon teaches herself to become efficient at her trade, because she knows that the more work she does, the more money she will take on Saturday.'

'A letter, this time from a male sufferer, brings out the essential weakness of the household servant, her unreliability. She cannot be depended upon and brings trouble and dismay into the household she is supposed to help, and the root of this is that coercive discipline cannot be employed as in a factory, but only moral pressure, and the girl has been very defectively educated on this point in the majority of cases.

'Too often the servant is absolutely indifferent to her duties, and recognises no obligation to treat her mistress as well as she herself expects to be treated, and the household is upset for the day. And too often, this discomfort penetrates into the business life of the husband.'
But the life of the servant girl was often a hard one, or even worse. It is not difficult to guess at the circumstances which led to a suicide reported that year in the *Hull Daily Mail* of a servant girl at Eastrington who threw herself into the Ouse. Her letter to her parents was read out by the Goole Coroner:
'I expect you will know that I have left H----s, but it was not my doing at all. It was the son's, but he had a letter from you this morning saying I had to go to you, and I told him I was not going, as I dare not face Father, and I know how strict you are. Mrs H. called me for not doing my work, but I could not help it. I could not give my mind to it. I can't take another place, so I think I will do away with myself. I have been a lot of trouble to you both and this will be the end.'
'I am very sorry, but George told me plainly that he was not going to pay if aught happened to me, and if he won't, nobody else will. I hope this will learn him a lesson as I was never willing. I will say goodbye to all of you. When you get this I shall not be alive. Blame him. He has driven me to it. There is a box and umbrella at Selby station.' What pathos lay in that final sentence.'

Went with Elsie, Gertie and Doris to the Alexandra Theatre October 26th, 1907, to see 'Sunday' with Sybil Walsh as Sunday.

There was a full house at the 'Alex' to see this old-fashioned drama of the Wild West. The star was Sybil Walsh, a favourite of the Edwardian stage, who played Sunday, the heroine of Silver Creek, named after the day of the week on which she had been born.

The Alexandra was known as the home of melodrama in Hull. Its high tower was a familiar landmark, with its revolving searchlight flashing out into the night. But apparently masters of ships on the Humber, confused by a light which did not appear on their charts, complained to the authorities at Trinity House, and the theatre management was ordered to remove the offending beacon. At the time the Alexandra Theatre had the largest stage of any theatre in the North of England; it featured a secret trap-door from which, at Christmas-time, the pantomime demon would dramatically appear in a flash of magnesium smoke.

If the Alex rated in class a little behind the Grand Opera House and the Theatre Royal, it certainly matched them in splendour, the auditorium richly decorated in red and gold, and its ornate ceiling lit by clusters of electric lamps – the Grand was still gas-lit. One advantage that the Alex enjoyed over its rivals was that the patrons were allowed to smoke during the performance, the large glass roof being slid back to let in fresh air.

There were two prices for seats in the 'pit', the normal one, and a limited number of others priced at a discount of sixpence or ninepence for customers who were prepared to queue for them. This was known as going 'early doors', and it was an expression commonly used in Hull on other occasions too – 'Be there early doors' was another way of saying, 'Don't be late'

Half-term holiday Monday November 4th, 1907. Went to the Exhibition with Ted in the afternoon; Gertie on the 13th, Tom on 16th, Charles on 21st, Tom on 25th and 28th, with Muriel Middlebrook on 7th & and on Saturday, the last day of the Exhibition, had tea there with Hector Darby

What a magnet the Exhibition was for Dorothy – eight visits in six weeks The big attraction that year was the Viennese Orchestra under Herr Julian Kandt. This was the programme on one of the evenings:

March - *Children of the Regiment*
Waltz - *Girls of Baden' (Kandt)*
Tragic Overture - *Maximilian Robispierre*
Song - *When Shadows Gather*
Serena - *Nicoise*
Selection from *Carmen*
Selection from *The Chocolate Soldier*
Valse Lente - *Royale*
Song - *Until*
Finale - *Slavonic Rhapsody*

Despite the tremendous popularity of the German and Austrian bands in the early years of the century, 1914 saw the end of them as far as English audiences were concerned. They never performed here again after the Great War.

Went to the Fair with Tom October 15th, 1907. Went in Bostocks and had a lovely time.

Most people who spent their youth in Hull have recollections of the annual Fair. For the young at heart it was a week of excitement and pleasure, while the kill-joys saw it as a event fraught with temptations and dangers, and the local shopkeepers complained about all the unpaid bills which followed in its wake. The rate-payers of Newington resigned themselves to a week of crowds, noise and dirt and an influx of doubtful characters into the neighbourhood. But Hull Fair made its impact on the whole of the East Riding, and was an event which nobody could ignore.

The Fair was held in Walton Street each October, almost on the Dentons' doorstep, and whilst Jabez and Clara no doubt did their best to give it a wide berth, the younger members of the family were drawn to it as iron filings to a magnet. The annual fair usually heralded the arrival of Autumn, but that year the *Hull Daily Mail* reported, 'The weather has been kind to Hull Fair, which has passed under most pleasant auspices. Starlit evenings have spread their beautiful canopies over the flare and revelry of Walton Street.'

Flare and revelry were apt descriptions. The scene at night was garishly lit by the paraffin flares and electric lights of the shows and roundabouts. Above the noise of the steam organs blaring out Souza marches, there arose the hubbub of the milling crowd and the shouts and laughter of excited youngsters. To them the Fair was an annual excuse for rowdy horse-play, as gangs of youths pursued squealing girls with their 'tickling brushes' and 'water-squirts'.

There were rides of every kind, from the stomach-turning lurch of the shamrocks, standing first on one end, and then the other, to the gentler roll of the gondolas and the undulating merry-go-round of the carousel's painted horses. Raising you on high, above the hurly-burly of the fairground were the Giant Dipper and the Big Wheel, or you could survey the scene at your leisure from the top of the Lighthouse climbing up the inside stairs, and sliding helter-skelter down the outside on a coconut mat. The cake-walks and the wiggle-woggles agitated to the sound of the newest ragtime music.

The showmen had many ways of wheedling the pennies out of the fair-goer's pocket. There were sideshows to amaze the credulous, the bearded lady, the fat lady, the two-headed calf, or the performing fleas; there were opportunities to win tawdry prizes on the hoop-la stalls, by knocking over heavily weighted coconuts with wooden balls, or demolishing a row of cans with a powder puff. Outside the boxing booth ugly pugilists with broken noses and cauliflower ears went through the motions of boxing, and the barker challenged any likely lad who could last three rounds with one of them to win a fiver.

The length of Walton Street was lined with stalls selling fruit, coconuts, pomegranates, brandy-snap, toffee-apples, and nougat, a Hull Fair confection so 'chowy' that it pulled the fillings out of your teeth. Some of the householders on Walton Street made a small annual windfall by letting out their front gardens to the fortune-tellers, all claiming to be the 'Original Gipsy Rose Lee', and others cashed in on the niffy state of the public toilets by making their private w.c. available for a small charge.

The Bostock and Wombwell's Menagerie which Dorothy so enjoyed was one of the big attractions of the Fair. For threepence the show offered, to quote the *Hull Daily Mail*, 'many novelties and unique animals never before seen in a travelling menagerie. The numerous carriages contain, among other specimens of the forest and jungle, the finest and largest lions of all ages, tigers, leopards, bears, hyenas, wolves, jaguars, a wagon-load of monkeys, and beautiful aviaries of foreign birds. There are three lion-tamers with this great show who give daily performances with all classes of wild animals. There are also elephants, camels, dromedaries for children to ride on, and the proprietors have just purchased, at enormous expense, Mr. Kenneth Clark's Olympia prize-winning team of Suffolk horses. Another great attraction is the extraordinary zoological novelty, a half-bred hybrid, half lion, half tiger.'

People in the first decade of this century were a good deal more credulous of stories about far-off lands than are their grandchildren, brought up in an age of television and world-wide holidays. Few of our grandparents' generation had ever left their native shores, let alone explored the wilds of Africa and other corners of the British Empire. This fanciful article in the *Hull Times* was, no doubt, swallowed unquestioningly by most of its readers:

'Few men, no matter of what race, have undergone such remarkable adventures and experiences as Mr. John Boyes, the well-known explorer and ivory trader, who is a native of Hull, and, after being for eight years hidden away in Darkest Africa, is visiting his native city. Our reporter interviewed Mr. Boyes and was given some interesting stories of the adventures of this intrepid big-game hunter and explorer.

"Mr. Boyes is 35 years of age, a keen-visaged, shrewd man, alert and intelligent, and one who loves to combine business with pleasure. This daring sportsman, who has spent practically the whole of his life in the depths of jungles in pursuit of big-game, claims to have shot over 400 elephants.

"When 13 years of age, Mr. Boyes started a roving career by going to sea, and since then he has been a globe-trotter. After service with the

Royal Navy Reserve for some time, he decided to view fresh fields by going to Africa. In 1896, therefore, he left Hull and journeyed to the Dark Continent, and at the time he had no idea of the stirring adventures that were to be experienced by him.

"First he went through great privations in the Matabele campaigns, and after this he made his way to British East Africa. The country thereabouts was practically unknown, and he was the first white man to be seen by the natives. Whilst engaged out there big-game shooting, Mr. Boyes came into contact with many tribes of savages and cannibals. He 'knocked about' with different tribes, and after getting to know their ways, was made 'King of the Kiyuki' (Kikuyu), a particularly warlike tribe around British East Africa. For three years he enjoyed the title of King, and had command of 5,000 warriors, but, owing to difficulties with the British Government, resigned his regal position and returned to England in 1902."'

Left off school on Thursday night, December 19th 1907. Prizes distributed by Mrs. Atkinson. I won the English prize. Played a pianoforte solo. Tom was there and came home with us.

When Councillor Mrs. T. Beecroft-Atkinson made the presentation at Aston High School speech day, Dorothy walked up to receive the English prize. *The Hull Daily Mail* reported the prize-giving, publishing the full list of students who had been successful in the Royal Academy of Music and the Royal College of Music exams, as well as the school prize-winners. Editors of the provincial press knew that 'names sell newspapers' and Dorothy had the satisfaction of seeing hers in print twice in the same column, as the winner of the English prize, and as one of the music pupils who entertained the guests, whose 'difficult pianoforte solos were accomplished with care, their efforts being reward with deserved applause'.

Went on Boxing Day to the Grand Theatre with Father, Nellie, Charles and Tottie to see 'Little Bo-Peep'.

The pantomime on Boxing Day was a Christmas tradition. The *Hull Daily Mail* reported that there was not a vacant seat: 'it was a house such as artistes love to play to. Everybody was determined to be merry, and every joke "told".' The audience, sated with Christmas fare, were obviously not hard to please, and were prepared to laugh at anything.

The critic conceded that the show was 'not of the first order', 'but it served to brighten the lives of those who saw it'. He could not, however, forbear to raise a question-mark against the performance of Mr. J.W. Groves, playing the part of Baron Hardup, whose act was deemed 'in need of a little blue pencil'. Full marks, however, for the transformation scene and the harlequinade, which closed the pantomime in time-honoured fashion.

The young lady included in the party was Tottie, otherwise Marie Dowson, a cousin of Jabez's. Truth to tell, the Dentons thought the Dowsons were a bit common, and sniggered at them behind their backs: Dorothy, however, made a friend of Tottie, and she was loyal to their friendship all her life. And it must be said that the Dentons were usually circumspect in their dealings with their Dowson cousins, for I think they knew of a skeleton somewhere in the Denton family cupboard.

All families have their 'dark secrets' and the Dentons were no exception. Reading through Dorothy's diaries, it is strange how seldom Clara accompanied her husband and children on family outings. The reason, which I learned many years later, was that Clara had a drink problem – what unhappiness drove her to seek solace in the Brandy bottle I do not know, but as the years went by she became more addicted. In the days when Dorothy was writing her diarys, her mother was within a few years of the end of her life.

1908

16th January, 1908 – Teddie commenced school at Miss Knowles.

About time too The lad was 7½ years old. I think Clara 'babied' her last-born, treating him as a delicate child and insisting on sending him to a private school. Edward Ernest Denton, whose godfather was Mr. E.E. Heslewood, Resident Secretary of the Yorkshire Insurance Company, was born on St. Swithin's Day, 15 July, 1900. It was customary for little boys to be dressed in frocks like their sisters until they were about four years old. At that age, they were 'breeched' and put into trousers. Photographs of Teddie as a small boy show him in the traditional sailor's outfit with square jack-tar's collar and knee-length breeches – Edwardian children tended to be dressed like smaller versions of their elders.

Received certificate for passing music examination at the Assembly Rooms, 27th January 1908. Maudie sang.

Modest though her achievement was, a pass in the Lower Division of the Royal Academy of Music exams, it was for Dorothy, none the less, a tangible reward for two years of study. Perhaps more important than the framed certificate was the achievement of a skill which would give many hours of pleasure to herself, her family and her friends. I am sure that Jabez would have been proud of his daughter and have felt that the money he had spent on her further education had been not been wasted.

Went with Father and Nellie to see 'The Gay Gordons' at the Grand Theatre, February 25th, 1908. Zena Dare as Peggy Quainton and Stanley Brett, (Seymour Hicks' brother) as Angus Graeme.

As a purveyor of syrupy, cliché-ridden prose, our local theatre critic excelled himself this week:
'The *Gay Gordons* are back, with the part of Peggy Quainton filled by Miss Zena Dare. Nothing more dainty and fresh and natural can be conceived than Miss Dare's interpretation of the millionaire's daughter,

determined not to be married for her dollars. Her disposition is so transparently honest, sunny and pleasure-loving, that she imparts her vivacity to the house, who follow her fortunes with the greatest delight. Miss Dare fills the part finely, and her wooing by Angus Graeme (Mr. Stanley Brett) makes a delightful stage episode. The incident of the Bond Street girls parading and singing in early Victorian costume made a pleasant feature in a play where one scene succeeds another with bewildering rapidity. The costumes are both beautiful and elaborate, and the play is in every respect well mounted. Those who wish for a genuine evening's amusement can do no better than repair to the Grand.'

With what decorum the theatrical world conducted itself in 1908. Whatever may have happened back-stage, to all outward appearances the theatre wore a mantle of respectability. The curtain never rose until the audience had settled down – a series of sibilant 'hushes' soon settled the chatterers. Exit doors were fastened and late-comers were obliged to wait until the end of the act before claiming their seats. The Edwardians loved their theatre and regarded as a boor anybody who interfered with the illusion created by the actors.

Gertie and I went to a concert at the Boys' Club on March 16th 1908. G. Cargill and S. Peacock and others gave a 'Coon' entertainment.

Face-blacking and performance of nigger-minstrel shows were still the vogue in Edwardian days. G.H. Elliott, the 'Chocolate-Coloured Coon', with his popular song, *Lily of Laguna*, was all the rage, and his act was widely copied. At the seaside the concert parties with their elegant songs were replacing the old minstrel shows, but the public still loved to see a 'blacked-up' artiste with his banjo rendering the old plantation songs, *Way Down upon the Swanee River* or *My Old Kentucky Home*.

There were no sensitive feelings to be hurt in 1908 – no race relations to worry about. Children still played with golliwogs, and the peoples of the far-flung parts of the Empire were referred to as 'His Majesty's dusky subjects'. Englishmen sang *Rule Britannia* and really believed that she did.

Nellie and I went down to the station and saw General Baden-Powell arrive by motor car and review the Boys' Brigade, 6.30 March 17th, 1908, and went with Father to see 'Maritana' - Moody Manners, at the Grand.

Dorothy was always prepared to turn out to see such popular figures as General Baden-Powell, the hero of the siege of Mafeking, and the founder of the Boy Scouts. B.P. had at the time recently launched the Boy Scout movement, an ideal born out of the success of a camp for boys of every class of society, which he had held in Dorset the previous summer. He had just written a book, *Scouting for Boys*, and his visit to Hull probably had in mind the publicising of his book. Boy-scouting, and later Girl-Guiding, reflected the idealism of the age, with its encouragment of clean and healthy living for young people; it was to elevate its founder into a world figure.

Celebrities of the stage, and people in the news, even before the days of the tabloid press, attracted more attention than the politicians. The biggest political issue of the day was Votes for Women, but it cannot have appealed to Dorothy, who makes no mention in her diaries of the activities of the Suffragettes. These militant women had their followers in Hull, and the *Hull Daily Mail*, advising that an open-air meeting on Corporation Field was to be held, gave the warning: 'The Suffragettes are far too experienced on public speaking to be deterred by fear of breaking the law, and it would be a rash man who tries a fall with them.'

In West Hull there were 3,000 widows and spinsters who were on the register for municipal elections, but had no vote in parliamentary elections. But the women in Dorothy's circle were not very politically-minded, and presumably the lack of a vote was of less importance to them than the latest Moody-Manners production at the Grand.

Mother and I went to see Vesta Tilley at the Palace, April 3rd. Programme also included the Four Magnanis and Japanese acrobats.

One of the rare occasions when Dorothy went to the theatre with her mother: Clara preferred music-hall entertainment to the 'improving' type of performance that Jabez favoured for his family. The Palace Theatre of Varieties was on Anlaby Road and almost within walking distance of the Denton home. Most music-halls gave shows twice-nightly, but the Palace, which attracted the top artistes of the day, staged only one evening performance from 7.30 to 10.30 pm, so to make the theatre pay the crowds had to be pulled in. By arrangement with the North Eastern Railway, special late trains were laid on to all the outlying districts, even as far away as Bridlington and York. Patrons taking their bicycles to the theatre were allowed to leave them in a special rack under the supervision of an attendant for one penny per machine.

Vesta Tilley was one of the great stars of the music-hall in her role as 'Piccadilly Johnnie' and the public loved her, although J.B. Priestley, who saw her in his youth, wrote that 'these male impersonators, who never looked or sounded like the soldiers and sailors they pretended to be, suffocated me with boredom, while all around me were enraptured'. But the *Hull Daily Mail* theatre critic had no such reservations:

'Vesta Tilley at the Palace last night revelled in a real Yorkshire welcome. Repeatedly she was recalled, and, in all, she indulged her audience at the first house to four songs. Unsatisfied, they pleaded vociferously for a fifth selection, but it was not forthcoming. Vesta Tilley's latest creations, *When the Right Girl comes along*, and *Good Luck to the Girls who love the Soldiers*, were received with the utmost delight. In the first song she appeared as a young dandy, and in the second as a red-coated soldier, entering the stage smoking a cigar. The audience laughed heartily at her correct imitation of a swaggering 'Tommy Atkins'. Her other two songs were *The Seaside Sultan*, and the old favourite, *Following in Father's Footsteps*.

'Though Vesta Tilley is the "star" this week, the remaining turns were decidedly attractive. This is particularly so of the Four Magnanis. Their novelty, "The Musical Barbers", introduces a barbers' shop where they play musically on razors, strops, shaving-pots, barbers' chairs and barbers' poles. Their rendering of *Miserere* was a very able performance. Yamamoto and Miss Koyoshi also deserve special notice. They are daring equilibrists, the young lady performing feats that almost take one's breath away.'

Music-hall turns were essentially of a popular nature: the songs were whistled by errand-boys, and the catch-phrases echoed in every factory and workshop. The programmes were made up of sentimental or comic songs, acrobats, jugglers, male and female impersonators, and comic sketches, as well as performing animals, conjurers or ventriloquists. The jokes were down to earth, about mothers-in-law, lodgers, pawnbrokers, beer, kippers, seaside landladies, unpaid bills and unfaithful husbands and wives – honest vulgarity, but never 'sick' jokes. There was jeering at foreigners and blatant jingoism.

Dorothy failed to mention it in her diary, but, according to the *Mail*, at the end of the live entertainment, the bioscope presented a film of the

1908.

New Year's day, Joan's Birthday. Ted & I went to tea. James & Ted & I went to Biz. Went with mother and Nellie to the matinee of Bluebeard Jan: 7th. Very good. Oxford, Brett & others were well Princess Hilda Stanchin. Spent the evening at May Leonards. Jan 14th. Ted commenced school at Miss Fooks. Jan 16th. Went to V & B Lamplug no 90. First drive January 22nd. Came home with Gertie & G. at 3 o'clock

Went to Andrews for the evening Sunday 26th Jan. Introduced to Miss H Stanchin who was playing in "Bluebeard" at the Royal. Received Certificate for Passing music exam at the Assembly Room Jan 27 Maundi say. Went with Father & Nellie to see "The Gay Gordons" at Grand Theatre February 25th 08. Zena Dare as Peggy Saunton and Stanley Brett (Seymour Hicks Brother) as Angus. Graeme. Dorothy Monkman also there.

Went to Mrs Lambert's Birthday party on February 28th 08. Becci and I went to May's to tea Saturday March 14th Gertie and I went to a Concert at the Boys Club on March 16th 1908. E. Cargill, G. Peacock, + others gave a coon entertainment. Mother & I went to town for the afternoon on Saturday, March 21st Nellie & I went down to the Station & saw General Baden Powell arrive by motor car & review the boy brigade. 6-30 March 27th & then we went to Father to see "Mentana" Moody Manners co. Grand

Nellie & Father went to see Vesta Tilley at the Palace April 2nd 08 Mother & I went to see Vesta Tilley April 3rd. Programme also included Musical Barbers & Japanese acrobats. Went with Gertie to Hymn's Sports. Wet afternoon. Mrs Feldman gave prizes April 4th 08 Went to see Living Pictures arranged by Mrs Russell at the Lecture Hall with Olga Watson April 9th. Gertie & I went in held Old Café with George Cargill & D Bradley. Saturday April 11th.

Nellie & Father went to see Vesta Tilley at the Palace April 2nd 08 Mother & I went to see Vesta Tilley April 3rd. Programme also included Musical Barbers & Japanese acrobats Went with Gertie to Hymn's Sports. Wet afternoon. Mrs Feldman gave prizes April 4th 08 Went to see Living Pictures arranged by Mrs Russell at the Lecture Hall with Olga Watson April 9th Gertie & I went in held Old Café with George Cargill & D Bradley Saturday April 11th

Octagon Jan 13th. Went to Reserve & Rivelino Res. won 6-1 Auntie Nellie & I went to Hinnamaelor Jan 16th

Mother Father & I went to the Palace. "Seymour Hicks & Gladys Cooper in Papa's Wife. Sammy Shields in Football. on January 17th. Auntie, Doris & I went to see Her Path of Sorrow at the Alexandra Jan 18 Went to City V Bristol on Thursday Jan 19th cup tie won 1-0 Sat. Jan 21. City V Lillian drew 0-0 Went to the Palace with Mo 25th. Jan 27 City V Chatham Sat Feb 4. Cup tie City won 1-0. Allyn D came over to tea. Went to Palace with Mrs Sheele Victoria Monks.

Pages from Dorothy Denton's Diary.

Grand National. It was shown only 24 hours after the race had been run, and that, in 1908, was no mean achievement.

Went with Gertie to Hymers' Sports, April 4th, 1908. A wet afternoon. Mrs. Feldman gave the prizes.

Cousin Gertie was the most attractive of the Fenner girls, an exceptionally pretty girl, and a great flirt. Wet or fine, Dorothy and Gertie would have enjoyed their afternoon among the boys at Hymers' Sports. Dorothy's brother, Charles, was then a sixteen-year old in his last year at school, and Gertie's brother, Jack, was in the same form as Charles. The two boys were firm friends. A few years later, when Jack was going through the hell of life in the trenches with the East Yorks, he wrote to Charles and advised him not to join the infantry. Charles took his cousin's advice and joined the East Riding Yeomanry, serving with them in Egypt.

In 1908 Hymers College was still a comparatively new school, not yet established twenty years. Set in the leafy neighbourhood of the former Botanic Gardens, the red-brick buildings made a congenial setting for a school sports day. Hymers was regarded as Hull's leading school, eclipsing the 400-year old Grammar School, and the well-to-do sent their sons there to be educated.

This year, however, Sports Day had been arranged a bit too early in the year to expect good weather. It poured all the afternoon, or, as the *Hull Daily Mail* apologetically put it: 'climatic conditions were not all that could have been wished for, but the annual sports in connection with Hymers College did not fail to provide enjoyment for all who witnessed them.'

The spectators, damp and chilled as they were, had their moment of fun. It was reported that: 'Some adventurous spirits, observing the approach of a malignant shower, scrambled over the fence separating the railway line from the grounds, and took up a comfortable position in some railway carriages conveniently placed opposite the finishing line. They were not destined to stay there long, however, for an engine silently arrived on the scene, and it was not until it was within a yard of the carriages that it was noticed. The adventurous ones beat a hasty retreat back to their rightful place, amidst the maledictions of the driver and fireman, and the laughter of the crowd.'

Went to see Living Pictures arranged by Mrs. Russell at the Lecture Hall, April 10th, 1908.

They had been called 'living pictures' since the days when they had first been shown at Randall Williams' side show at Hull Fair, the show which had sensationally burned down the previous year. At the time of this entry in Dorothy's diary, the cinema had not yet become an entertainment in its own right, and the bioscope, a crude form of moving pictures, was usually a short presentation tagged on to the end of a theatrical performance. J.B. Priestley recalls that he found these jerky films so uninteresting that he seldom stayed on to see them.

But for a year or two the Circus, situated on Anlaby Road, next to the Palace, had been showing Globe Animated Pictures. The *Hull Daily Mail* reported:

'Mr. Edward Emerson, Manager of the Circus, has presented another series of Globe Animated Pictures for his patrons this week. Entire changes are made in the films each week and are greatly appreciated by the large audience who assemble nightly. Unfortunately for Mr. Emerson, the electric light failed on Monday night, shortly before the completion of the first programme, and, to the disappointment of his audience, occurred during a sensational picture, *The Youthful Hero*. The delay did not diminish the enthusiasm displayed by the juveniles, who cheered lustily when the young hero rescued two children from a burning house. Mr. Emerson did not delay the programme longer than necessary and the breakdown was soon remedied and the entertainment continued.'

As the craze for moving pictures began to grow, businessmen soon noticed the trend, and there was a rush for licences under the new Cinematograph Act. Local premises mushroomed all over the city, and a number of shops in the centre were converted for the purpose of showing films. The Electric Theatre in Whitefriargate offered, Amusements and Animated Pictures for twopence, whilst rivals in Market Place, Picton and Persee's Animated Pictures, offered a similar entertainment for only a penny.

When purpose-built cinemas began to be built a few years later, the Dentons profited very nicely. Jabez Denton and his next-door neighbour at 421, Anlaby Road, sold their houses to developers to build the West Park Cinema; it opened its doors in 1914, a few weeks before the outbreak of the First World War. The Dentons moved a few houses back to Antrim Lodge at 409, Anlaby Road.

Edwardian ladies and gentlemen at Bridlington's Floral Pavilion.

The sands at Filey.

Gertie and I went to Field's Cafe with George Cargill and Don Bradley, Saturday April 11th, 1908.

So typically Edwardian, Hull's popular city-centre rendezvous survived, almost unchanged, for three more decades until the May night in 1941 when the German bombers destroyed it, along with the rest of King Edward Street.

In Dorothy's day Field's Café, then in Savile Street, was the favourite haunt of city shoppers, commercial travellers, and middle-class ladies with time on their hands. It was the place where friends met among the potted palms at small tables set in alcoves, to be served by waitresses in black dresses with white caps, collars and cuffs, with afternoon tea. The rattle of crockery sounded cheerfully over the hum of conversation, at times all but drowning out the valiant efforts of the ladies' orchestra playing selections of light music. Toasted muffins dripping with butter appeared at the table on covered silver dishes, and tall cake-stands, loaded with sinfully rich cakes, were set unbidden before the patrons, a temptation few could resist. And there was the reviving brew, with hot water to replenish the teapot and keep the tea drinking going all afternoon.

Bright animated conversation in a cheerful atmosphere whiled away the afternoon, until one suddenly realised it was time to go. A threepenny-bit slipped under the plate for the waitress, and then a dash to catch the tram home – Happy memories of Field's Octagon Café, and the many cinema cafés that flourished in Hull a couple of generations ago.

Mother, Nellie and I arrived at Brid, April 16th for Easter. Went on the Parade with Gertie at night, and also next day, Good Friday. Sunday morning went to Chapel with Doris. Easter Monday fine. Went on Parade with Mother in the morning and Teddie in the afternoon. Mother, Father and I came home Thursday April 24th, 1908.

It was the birth of the Easter Parade. The Edwardians invented it, and the song-writers wrote songs about it. The season at Bridlington began at Easter and carried on right through to October. April was never a month to trust, especially on the East coast, but this year the weather might have been worse. The *Bridlington Free Press* wrote: 'Monday was the grand opening day of the season at the Royal Prince's Parade, and, when one recalls the fact that only a few days ago people were busy predicting a White Easter, it was certainly almost cheering that on the opening day there was something like Spring sunshine, even though followed by a keen wind across the bay in the evening.'

Visitors to Bridlington early in the season were often aware of the 'keen, cool rush of the air' when the wind was off the North Sea. Those hardy ladies who braved the stiff sea breeze in their fashionable outfits, holding tight to their Easter bonnets as they walked up and down the sea-front, frozen to the bone, but grimly determined to show off their finery, were demonstrating that peculiarly Edwardian virtue of 'making a toil of a pleasure'. Easter was the time for new clothes, and Dorothy listed hers in her diary – a saxe-blue costume, white muslin dress, blue hat and shoes, and she wrote: 'I put my hair up May 10th, but took it down again.'

That Easter the Floral Pavilion had been spruced up for the season. The *Bridlington Free Press* offered 'a special word of praise for the exceedingly beautiful display of flowers, plants, large palms, ferns and creepers, which were so tastefully arranged on the platform, and which gave such a pleasing and effective finish to the whole scene'.

The music of the newly formed Municipal Orchestra was under the direction of Mr. Norfolk Megone and was 'pronounced to be a success from the very outset, providing a fine rich haul of musical delight'. On the Monday night Miss Elsie Hope, soprano, sang *The Jewel Song* from *Faust (Were I but a royal lady, he would indeed adore me)*, forever after, one of Dorothy's favourite operatic airs.

Mother, Father, Charles and Ted went to Bridlington for Whitsuntide. Whit Sunday, my birthday, gold curb from Father. Went to West Park on Whit Monday. Nellie and I stayed at Aunt Jinnie's. On Tuesday went for a drive around Anlaby, Willerby and Cottingham.

Dorothy's 18th birthday. Father's gift was a gold curb, a 15-carat gold curb bracelet from Larard's in Savile Street (£1.17.0). Father gave it to her before he and Clara and the boys set off to Bridlington for the Whit weekend. Why Dorothy and Nellie didn't go with their parents is not clear, but Jabez declined to leave his teenage daughters alone in the house; 18-year-old girls in Edwardian times were deemed in need of protection, so the girls stayed with Aunt Jinnie and their Fenner cousins.

Whit Monday in West Park – a fine day would draw out the crowds, and there would have been people sunning themselves on deck chairs, or sitting on the grass around the bandstand with a military band playing popular airs; couples with small children by the ornamental lake feeding bread crusts to the ducks, and ladies with large hats admiring trim flower beds, bright with Spring colour; elderly red-faced gentlemen huffing and puffing on the bowling greens; children chasing butterflies, playing noisily on the slides and swings, or climbing the old discarded ship's anchor, set up by the Corporation as a decoration, but always a target for nimble youngsters. Older boys indulged in forbidden games of football or cricket, keeping a wary eye open for the approach of 'Parkie'. By the park gates the old Italian hokey-pokey man would have been doing a good trade, scooping the bright yellow icecream into ha'penny cornets, or fat penny sandwiches. Poor children who had no pennies to spend satisfied their thirst with water from an iron cup secured by a chain to the fountain. For many of the people of Hull a day in the park was the nearest thing to a holiday they were able to enjoy. Not one family in four ever had a holiday away from the city – even a day at Hornsea or Withernsea was beyond their means.

Although Dorothy was a city girl, born and bred, she had a great love for the countryside, and, living as she did on the outskirts of the city, it was only a few minutes walk to the green fields and hedgerows of Haltemprice. Many people had bicycles – they were affordable at only £3 – and on summer weekends it was a common sight to see cyclists pedalling out to the woods at Hessle and returning with sheaves of bluebells hanging from their handlebars.

The countryside was at its best in the early days of this century, before encroaching suburbs and mass ownership of cars ruined it. Many of the roads around Hull which today carry streams of cars, buses and lorries were, in 1908, little more than country lanes. A lot of them were in a very rough condition, for, since the development of the railways, England's roads had suffered a benign neglect; they were still narrow and winding, and many of them were full of potholes. The Fenners had their own transport – not yet the new-fangled motor car, but a smart two-wheeled trap with a sturdy grey cob between the shafts. On Whit Tuesday Uncle Harry took the girls for a jaunt around the country through Anlaby, Willerby and Cottingham, villages which have now been virtually swallowed up by the city.

Older people recall days when the roads were almost empty of traffic, and the verges were overgrown with fern, wild roses and foxglove. In that late Spring day in 1908 the silence was broken only by the cooing of wood pigeons and the song birds in the woods, and the only traffic Harry Fenner and his party were likely to encounter was a slow moving farm wagon with its fragrant load of hay. Men with scythes were mowing the long sweet grass, and cattle grazed by the verges. As the old horse meandered quietly through the country lanes, the Denton and Fenner cousins chatted happily, enjoying the simple pleasures of a day in the country, and knowing the peace and tranquillity of an England that later generations could never hope to recapture.

Anlaby was then essentially a village, just a row or two of cottages, a few village shops, and a blacksmith's forge, with its centuries-old church standing on the gently rising ground. The Red Lion was then a real village pub, with sawdust on the floor and spittoons on the wall, and old men smoking twist in their clay pipes reached up to the narrow shelf above their heads for their glass of ale. Next to the pub was Harrison the joiner, who also served the community as its undertaker, and beyond his shop in Wilson Street, named after the family of the shipping line who owned most of the land, was the house of Mr. Sissons, the Hull paint manufacturer.

Bill Westoby, now well into his 80's, remembers the Sissons' mansion well:

'I used to cycle down the drive to the back door as a lad delivering the morning newspapers,' he says. 'Most mornings when I arrived there about 6.30 am, the kitchen windows were open, and large dinner-plate pies were cooling off on the sill. Didn't I look longingly at those pies – up at 4.30 am with no breakfast inside me, having cycled about six miles, I would dearly have loved to have knocked one of them back. I was 13 years of age, hungry on a winter's morning, and no breakfast until I got back home at eight o-clock.

'I only saw Mr. Sissons once – for that matter, he was the only person other than the butler I ever did see at the mansion, and that was one Christmas, when most people I served gave me my Christmas-box, anything from sixpence to half a crown, depending on how generous they were. I had received tips from all my other customers, but nothing from Mr. Sissons. I marched boldly up to the front door and pulled the bell-rope, and a rather plump gentleman in a morning coat with pin-striped trousers appeared. "Yes my boy, what is it that you require?" "I am your paper-boy, sir, and I wish you a Happy Christmas and a prosperous New Year." "Thank you, my boy, and my best wishes to you. Just stand there a moment." He turned and shouted to the back of the house, "John, are you there? I want you to come to the front door." When John arrived he put his hand into his pin-striped trousers and brought out a coin which he handed to the butler and instructed him, "John, give this to the boy." Mr. Sissons could have given it to me himself, but no, John the butler had to hand it over. All that going on, I thought, just for a measly shilling!'

Willerby was an even smaller village than Anlaby, little more than a single street running between rows of cottages leading to Castle Hill. The mental hospital, which was known to all and sundry in those days as 'Willerby Asylum', was on top of Castle Hill. It had been built there a decade earlier after the closing of Hull's old lunatic asylum in Argyle Street. Willerby had a chapel but no church, and the local Anglicans had to walk up Packman Lane to the church at Kirkella. The old Hull and Barnsley high-level railway passed through and above the village, and in 1908 its elevated station gave Willerby's few residents a convenient link with Hull. The Star Inn in Willerby enjoyed a reputation in those days for hospitality; the landlord served the hungry customer with big chunks of home-made bread and cheese, and he could help himself from the jar of pickled onions placed on the counter – a satisfying lunch for threepence. Food was incredibly cheap in Edwardian days – in the city cafés a portion of roast beef, mutton, or steak-and-kidney pie could he had for fourpence, with jam roll or rice pudding for an extra penny.

Uncle Harry steered the pony and trap down Castle Hill and along the Eppleworth Road into Cottingham, said by the locals to be the biggest village in England. It was an area known for its market-garden produce. The salad growers of Cottingham worked a fertile soil, made richer by the nourishment it received from the privies of its expanding neighbour. The older districts of Hull did not in those days have the benefit of flush water closets or main drains. The privy, which was located at the bottom of the yard, had to be emptied periodically by the men from the Corporation who shovelled the contents into metal tubs. These tubs were tipped into carts drawn by heavy horses, which then lumbered in the direction of Cottingham with their enriching cargoes, known euphemistically as 'night soil', although I have no doubt the men on the carts used the shorter Anglo-Saxon word for it. The *Hull Daily Mail* had a word to say on the subject: 'It is no secret that a great deal of the trouble over the night-soil question has for some time existed for the want of more roads in Hull. The carts may have left the city at a time acceptable to the authorities, but there have been constant complaints of carts passing through Cottingham at mid-forenoon. And this state of things has grown since Newington developed, and the night-soil carts from the second mile-stone on Hessle and Anlaby roads could not but come under the condemnation of the sanitary authorities. They had to go seven or eight miles round, when some new roads, such as Mr. Bricknell foreshadows, would have lessened the route by four or five miles.'

It was to be some years before the Council built the new roads, and one of them was Bricknell Avenue, the link road to Cottingham, which they named after their City Engineer. But by the time it was built in the 1920's, night-soil had ceased to be a problem; new deep sewers now diverted their soil-enriching contents into the Humber instead of it being spread on Cottingham's gardens.

Went to Bridlington with Nellie for the weekend Friday July 18th and came home on Tuesday 21st. On Saturday heard the Archbishop of York speak in the Pavilion.

The King's appointment that year of the Most Reverend Dr. Cosmo Lang as the Archbishop of York had been enthusiastically received. Dr. Lang was not a stranger to Bridlington and recalled that he had last been there twenty years before when, as a young curate, he had charge of a party of children from the slums of Leeds on a day's outing, and he contrasted the dignity and honour of today's visit with the frantic struggle he had had on the previous occasion to prevent his young charges, many of them seeing the sea for the first time, from drowning themselves:

'Today I can share with some degree the gratitude of thousands of people from our great cities, Leeds, Sheffield and Hull, for the benefits which Bridlington can give them in their search for holidays and health.' He told his civic hosts, 'You are in a real sense the guardians of a great trust, and I am sure I shall carry you with me when I say that I trust, as Mayor and Councillors, you are doing all you can to diminish the temptations of such a place . . . that everything is taken away that can bring shame, waste and extravagance, and turn their holiday from a blessing to a bane.' But the *Free Press.* revealed Bridlingtons naughty side:

'Harry William Boyd, a postcard dealer of Garrison Street, Bridlington, and his assistant Annie Collins were charged with offering for sale and exposing two obscene postcards on 5th July. Sgt. Brown said he had, while in uniform, purchased a set of six postcards from Miss Collins and had paid her sixpence. Two of them he had considered obscene and said to the young lady, "Don't you think these cards are unfit to be in the window?" She replied, "Well, no doubt they are nasty things. I didn't like them when they came, but what can I do? Mr. Boyd sent them and expects me to sell them."

Mr. Boyd said the cards were not obscene. "They depicted," he said, "a gentleman in ordinary civilian costume attempting to kiss a lady in a regulation bathing costume." There was a demand for them, and he had never had any complaints about the postcards he sold.

The Chairman of the Bench found the two postcards were obscene on account of their suggestiveness. Miss Collins would be fined one shilling, costs being remitted, and the male defendant would be fined 10/- with costs.'

But the misdemeanours of Harry Boyd and Annie Collins paled into insignificance in comparison with a case brought at the Grimsby Police Court the same month:

'The determination of the Grimsby police to protect the morals of Cleethorpes and its reputation as a resort was shown in the prosecution on Thursday of Joseph Miller, 46, described as a salesman, on a charge of vagrancy by exhibiting an indecent exhibition. The defendant had offered postcards for sale, some in the form of objectionable pictures, and others with a printed communication which ostensibly appeared to be an ordinary letter, but, read in a particular way, was a most filthy expression. The prosecution described it as one of the most vile cases ever brought to court. Wilson was sentenced to three months hard labour and ordered to pay 10/-, or do 14 days, for acting as a pedlar without a licence.' (*Hull Times*)

Went to Filey on Saturday August 29th, 1908 to Mrs. Pashley's in Rutland Street. Gertie came to stay with us Tuesday Sept. 8th. Came home from Filey on 16th. Wet day.

The first fortnight in September, the time for the Dentons' annual holiday in Filey, had come round again. As always, they stayed at the Pashleys' boarding house in Rutland Street, a homely establishment to be sure, but staying there was quite different from staying at Grandma's house in Bridlington – it felt more like a real holiday. And in the Dentons' opinion, there wasn't a finer resort in the whole world than dear old Filey. The sands were cleaner, firmer, and smoother, the sea calmer, the atmosphere more refined, and the people who stayed there of superior quality to those you met anywhere else. Sometimes, on her way down to the sands, Dorothy would pause and lean over the iron hand rail at the top of Cargate slip-way looking out to sea, and, for long minutes, stand drinking in the scene before her. This contemplation of Filey Bay on a summer morning gave her an enormous feeling of happiness. The sun sparkled on a dead-calm sea, and small waves washed gently over the smooth yellow sand. A few yards from the shore-line, in waist-deep water, fishing cobles bobbed gently at anchor, and fishermen in waterproof thigh boots waded out, ferrying their passengers in high-wheeled carts. Children, with their clothing hitched up and tucked-in, played by the water's edge with spade and bucket or scooped small creatures from the pools with their shrimping nets. In the shelter of the sea-wall family parties gathered around the bathing tents; groups of well-behaved children played together, and some of the more patrician families had a governess, or even an Indian *ayah* to look after the little ones.

Above the promenade rows of Georgian houses, where the better-off stayed, overlooked the Crescent Gardens, with their trim lawns, and beds of late summer blooms, and after Sunday morning church the soberly dressed visitors strolled the lawns exchanging polite greetings with friends and neighbours.

The holidaymakers of Edwardian days ate well. With abundant leisure and no office to attend, Jabez could afford to linger over his breakfast. There was no such nonsense as a Continental breakfast, and Mrs. Pashby provided her guests with enough solid food to satisfy the most demanding of appetites. She and her daughter would bring to the breakfast table dishes of crisp, curly bacon, fried or scrambled eggs, fat sausages and kidneys swimming in gravy, or fresh Filey bloaters. But before tackling this rich fare, the Edwardian breakfaster would first make a lining for his stomach with creamy porridge, and only then proceed to fill his plate with the cooked victuals. And if by any chance at the end of all that he was still hungry there would be scones, thick with butter and jam, or home-made marmalade, and cups of tea or coffee. And this was just to start the day – the main meals were even more fortifying.

After breakfast Jabez and his family enjoyed a walk down to the Brig, the sloping rocks covered with enormous boulders, running fully half a mile out to sea, forming a natural breakwater and sheltering the bay. Sometimes town-dwellers who had not learned respect for the sea ventured recklessly on to the slippery rocks, defying the restless sea to move them, and seldom a year passed but some foolhardy soul paid for his daring with his life. A memorial tablet affixed to a rock recorded the drowning in 1873 of Charles Paget, M.P. for Nottingham, and his wife, when a freak wave swept them off the rocks. It served to warn the careless visitor, and Jabez always drew the attention of the family to its grim message. The contours of the Brig formed deep green rock-pools, where children waded in search of small crabs and star-fish, while anglers, poised on the rocky platforms, fished for the mackerel which came into the bay in September.

On the sands a semi-circle of deckchairs around a wooden platform was the open-air stage on which Andy Caine and his troup of pierrots entertained, the children sitting on a mat in front of the stage. And competing for their pennies were the Punch-and-Judy man and the donkey-rides. The donkeys at Filey wore bells around their necks like Alpine cattle, and, as the boy herded them down to the sands each morning, the tinkle of their bells as they passed reached the ears of the

A Filey which has changed little over the years.
Above: the Bay from the south. Below: the Promenade.

breakfasting Dentons, and one of the children would call out 'The donkeys are going down,' urging the elders to hurry up and get down to the beach.

The grass on the cliff top was coarse and springy where the path led to the coastguard station, and if you knew where to look you could still see the remains of an ancient Roman camp. There were winding paths to be explored in the Ravine, dark and mysterious where the trees overarched thickly. In the evenings concert parties played in the Crescent Gardens, and audiences laughed at the gentle sophistry of Jack Millard, the resident 'humourist'.

The September days were always warm and sunny, and the nights soft and balmy. It was good to be alive and young in this most delightful of seaside resorts, the Filey of Dorothy's far-off youth.

Auntie, Elsie, Gertie and I went to London for five days Sept. 21st, 1908.

And that brief line is all that Dorothy wrote about the holiday she spent with her Aunt Jinnie and her cousins in London. I believe it must have been the first time Dorothy had been to London. Why, oh why, couldn't she have told us what she and her cousins did there?

They must have gone to London by train, for that was the only way for people to travel long distances in 1908. The North Eastern Railway offered excursion fares from Hull to London during the summer – a half-day excursion could be had for as little as five shillings and sixpence (27½p). The full return fare at a halfpenny a mile would have amounted to less than £1, and the journey to King's Cross took only a little longer than it does today. It may not have been quite the smooth, quiet journey of today's Inter-City trains, running silently on continuous-welded rail – it was wheels running over the gaps between the lengths of rail which made the the *diddly-da, diddly-da* sound, so familiar to the rail travellers of yesteryear, – but, even then, the old steam trains were capable of clocking up 60 or 70 miles an hour. At full speed the rhythmic click of the wheels on the metals, the noisy chattering as they crossed over the points, and the *whoosh* and shudder of a train thundering past on the opposite line all added to the excitement of travel by express train.

The carriages were old-fashionedly comfortable, well upholstered and clean, and quite free of litter and graffiti. But there was always a faint odour of dust and smoke lingering in the upholstery of the seats. If anybody opened the window, lowering the leather strap a few notches, black spots of soot and cinder fragments would most likely be blown into the compartment. On the main-line expresses the coaches were linked with a corridor running the length of the train, and each compartment, seating six (or eight with the arm-rests up), had a sliding door leading on to the corridor. On local trains the compartments held ten or more passengers, two rows facing each other, with no access to toilets. Stringnet luggage racks stretched over the passengers' heads, and below them were mildewed mirrors and sepia photographs advertising resorts on the line. Above the carriage doors hung the emergency chain, with the warning of a £5 fine for improper use. In winter the train was heated by steam pipes below the seats, and sometimes they gave off such an excess of heat that passengers complained of scorched ankles.

Once clear of Hull's western suburbs, the train passed through countryside little changed since the 19th century. A traveller in 1908 would have remarked that the wide expanse of the Humber between Hessle and Brough was a much busier waterway, with a procession of keels, barges and small ships passing up and down. On either side of the line stretched endless fields where horses still pulled the plough, and manual workers, men, women and children bent over manual tasks on the land. On the approach of the train, the noise sent scores of rabbits scampering for cover; cattle looked up impassively from their grazing in pastures covered in those days with wild flowers, and sometimes young horses would shy up in alarm and bolt round the paddock.

On wayside stations the milk churns rattled as the express thundered through, and country porters sweeping the station platforms leaned on their brushes to watch the London train pass. The roads were unbelievably quiet; nobody had yet travelled on them at speeds even half as fast as the train. At level-crossings in villages and small market-towns men with horses and carts waited patiently for the gates to open.

As the train approached the outskirts of London the scene gradually changed to the red bricks and modern architecture of suburbia, and soon the imposing buildings of the world's greatest capital came into sight. The high-roofed King's Cross station was filled with the hiss of escaping steam as the driver opened the valve and blew off his excess, and porters touted for custom, barrowing the passengers' bags to waiting taxis, well satisfied with a few coppers as a tip. All the areas round the main-line stations had plenty of family hotels; the Windsor for example, offered single rooms for three shillings a night, or doubles at five shillings, with *table d'hôte* breakfast at half-a-crown, and dinner at five shillings. The Palace Hotel offered bedroom (with electric light), service and breakfast at 5/6d a night.

The streets of the West End presented a scene no less lively than today. Most of the traffic was still horse-drawn, buses, cabs, carts and rullies, but an increasing number of motor-buses and electric trams were making their appearance. Rush hour in Piccadilly Circus or on Ludgate

Hill made the centre of provincial towns like Hull look like a village green. And for the country cousins there was the uniquely London experience of riding on an escalator into the bowels of the earth and making an exciting trip on the London Underground

The girls mingled happily with the thousands of visitors, window-shopping along Oxford Street, admiring the expensively priced jewellery in the shops in Bond Street, and gawping at finely dressed ladies, alighting from their carriages attended by liveried footmen on a leisurely morning's shopping in the West End. London was full of fashionably smart foreigners, Orientals dressed in their bejewelled robes with turbans and rich saris. Apart from Lascar sailors around the docks, dark-skinned foreigners were a rare sight on the streets of Hull.

That week in September, 1908, the West End theatres offered a rich choice of entertainment. *The Merry Widow* was still playing to packed houses at Daly's, the Duke of York's Theatre had J.M.Barrie's new play, *What Every Woman Knows*, with Gerald Du Maurier in the lead, and the D'Oyly Carte Opera Company presented *The Mikado* at the Savoy. Ada Reeve was starring in *Butterflies* at the Apollo, and James Forbes-Robinson appeared in the new thriller at the St. James', *The Passing of the Third Floor Back*. Most of these shows were later to come to Hull on their provincial tours, and the girls would undoubtedly have chosen to wait to see them at the Grand, rather than part with Father's hard-earned sovereigns on West End theatre prices. Vaudeville offered a chance to see the stars of the day at the Tivoli, where Harry Lauder, Little Tich, Wilkie Bard and George Robey were appearing, and the Victoria Palace advertised Maud Allan in her *Wonderful Classical Dances*, plus the novelty of the *Urbana Bioscope*.

Henry Wood was already in the second decade of his Promenade Concerts at the Queen's Hall – Monday's programme included Dvorak's overture *Carnaval*, Tchaikowsky's *Capriccio Italien*, César Franck's *Variations Symphoniques*, Schubert's *7th Symphony in C*, and Beethoven's *Egmont* overture. Madame Tussaud's Exhibition in Baker Street drew the crowds then as now, and tourists could admire the magnificent display of court dresses, the Hall of Tableaux and the Chamber of Horrors, and examine the newest addition of the season, a youthful Winston Churchill, who had that year been appointed President of the Board of Trade in Mr. Asquith's Liberal Government. The Zoological Gardens in Regent's Park claimed to house the finest collection of animals in the world, including a special exhibition of specimens from Australia and New Zealand, and living Birds of Paradise.

At night Aunt Jinnie may have treated her daughters and niece to an evening at the Trocadero in Piccadilly Circus, Lyon's famous Corner House, which offered an orchestral concert and a *table d'hôte* dinner at five-bob a head. But London was then, as it still is, a wonderful source of free entertainment, and Dorothy and her friends would have been limited only by the time they had available – Westminster Abbey, the British Museum, the National Gallery, the Guildhall – places where the visitor could wander about freely in those less turbulent days without a security guard in sight. There were still the narrow mediaeval alleyways and Wren's beautiful 17th-century churches to admire, views of the City of London that, after the night in 1940, would never be there again for Dorothy's grandchildren to see. There were pigeons to feed in Trafalgar Square, military bands to march in step with at the Changing of the Guard, acres of green in the Royal Parks, seats on the Embankment to watch the river craft, and perhaps to ride on one of them on a half-day excursion to the Tower or Greenwich. And I have no doubt that, as darkness fell, the girls would prevail on Jinnie to take them to Soho to see the 'naughty' sights. I can imagine Dorothy and Gertie nudging each other at the sight of a painted lady on a street corner, and speculating if she was 'one of those'.

How much excitement they crammed into those five days we shall never know, and more's the pity. Edwardian London was, I am sure, a subject on which Dorothy could have told us a great deal more than she did.

Mr. Darby buried 16th October 1908.

Funerals in Edwardian days were sombre affairs. The hearse was drawn by a black horse with a black plume fastened to its bridle. The darkly-suited mourners followed behind, four to a cab, each drawn by a black horse, and the procession set off at walking pace for the cemetery. The bearers, each carrying his black silk hat in the crook of his arm, walked in front of each cab, holding tightly to the horse's bridle.

As the cortège passed down the street passers-by would stand still, and the men and boys would doff their headgear; it was considered very bad form not to do so. Neighbours drew their curtains as a mark of respect on the day of the funeral and did not open them again until the cortège had passed out of the street.

Mr. Darby, who was the father of Hector Darby, one of Dorothy's earliest sweethearts, had been seriously ill for some time. For several days before he died the road outside his house in Cholmley Street had been covered with straw to deaden the sound of metal-rimmed wheels and horses' hooves on the cobbled street. Alternatively, tan chippings from Holmes' Tannery in Campbell Street could have been used for this purpose, but they were inclined to smell after they had been down for a day or two.

It was common practice in those days for the surface of roads outside hospitals, or places where quiet was essential, to be laid with wooden blocks, or wood setts as they were called. Years later when the roads were macadamised, the tarred wooden blocks, pitted with small stones, were dug up and sold off to the public to burn on their fires. They burned well enough, but with an acrid black smoke, and left a glutinous mess of melted tar to be cleaned off the grate next morning.

Went with Nellie and Tottie to see 'The Merry Widow' at the Grand on Nov. 10th, 1908. Clara Evelyn as the Widow, Basil Foster as Prince Dandillo. There at quarter to six, 5th row, early pit. Very good company. Absolutely packed.

This was the show that Hull had waited for months to see. *The Merry Widow* had taken the world by storm and was by far the most successful musical show for years. King Edward VII had seen it no less than four times during its West End run, but the public of Hull had only one week in which to see it. Dorothy and Nellie and Tottie made sure of good seats in the pit by joining the queue nearly two hours before curtain-up.

The theatre management announced in the *Hull Daily Mail*: 'A rumour has gained currency that all seats are already booked for the visit of *The Merry Widow*. Mr. Morton wishes to state that there are 3,500 bookable seats for the eight performances. Out of that number, little more than half have been taken up. Early application is, however, respectfully advised for the remaining good positions.'

The rapturous reception which the public of Hull gave *The Merry Widow* was not, however, echoed by the *Hull Daily Mail* theatre critic who wrote:

'*The Merry Widow* is bright enough, sparkling enough, clever enough. Musically it is far beyond any musical comedy we can call to mind. About the entire production there is a glittering elegance. And yet behind it all there lurks an atmosphere of unwholesomeness that we cannot but regret. From the very beginning a feeling of unhealthiness is given, and, as the piece progresses, becomes increasingly pronounced.

'The play opens in a scene in which a man is trying his utmost to persuade another man's wife to infidelity, and through two acts he pursues her until we finally see her fall into his arms. This is interest apart altogether from the affairs of the 'Merry Widow'. We meet this vivacious

Steamers unloading on to barges in Albert Dock, 1909.

The cabs and buses in Piccadilly Circus sorted themselves out without the help of policemen or traffic-lights.

lady surrounded by scores of adorers, all anxious to marry her – for her money, as she knows well. Really the widow is in love with a prince. This estimable person presently appears, very deeply under the influence of wine, and in this condition, among other passages of affection, he talks of his love, declares he will never tell her he loves her, and frequently puts himself as near to kissing her proffered, willing lips as it is possible to get without actual contact. Later the prince and the widow waltz, and of all the unwholesome aspects of the piece, this is the most gratuitously unwholesome. It is sensuousness carried to the extreme.

'The Merry Widow was received with many signs of enthusiasm by a crowded house, but it is probable that there were many who shared our view of it. Without approving of the part, it is still possible to say with what powers of fascination Miss Clara Evelyn impersonates the widow. She has some admirably written music to sing, and, since she possesses a voice of considerable charm and executive ability, her singing gives much pleasure. Miss Mary Grey is another singer of very effective songs. She represents the wife who is so unfortunate as to be trembling on the brink of temptation.

'Chief among the humourists of the piece is Mr. Lionel Victor in the part of Baron Popoff, the husband of the unfaithful lady. Mr Basil Foster is seen as the loose-living Prince Dandilo, with his bunch of special girls at a place known as *Maxim's* – it is he who accompanies the widow in the waltz. A number of other parts are adequately filled.'

If ever a piece was damned by faint praise, that was the fate of *The Merry Widow* at the hands of the *Mail* theatre critic. What, one wonders, would this worthy gentleman have to say about some of the productions which have graced the English stage since he last took up his pen? *O Tempora – O Mores!*

Went on board the s.s. Delphic in Albert Dock on Sunday Nov. 22nd, 1908 with Father.

Jabez enjoyed a Sunday morning walk on the Riverside Quay to view the shipping. He had no connection with the sea, but he was fascinated by ships. The *Delphic* was in the Albert Dock that Sunday morning and Jabez, in some manner, had received an invitation for himself and Dorothy to go aboard. Perhaps he had some contacts through the insurance world or, more likely, the officer of the watch, observing this gentleman and his 18-year-old daughter standing on the quayside, invited them on board to look around; he probably thought it would be nice to have a chat with the daughter.

The *Delphic* had arrived in Hull a fortnight before with a cargo of wool and passengers from Australia. She was a fair-sized ship, grossing 9,000 tons and built in 1893; she had put into Hull for a refit after discharging her cargo, and was due to sail for the Clyde in mid-December.

If the second, or third officer, or whoever was on watch, fancied the chance of a chat with a young lady, it was hardly surprising. He would seldom have a chance of female company in his profession. A life at sea in the early years of the century was hard and unrewarding. The *Delphic*'s Crew Agreements show that her first officer, with responsibilities second only to those of the captain, was paid the princely salary of £16 a month. But, if the mate felt hard done by, how could the lower ranks have felt? The stokers and trimmers, the lowest form of life aboard the ship, earned a miserable wage of £5 a month For this pittance they sweated naked in the bowels of the ship in tropical heat, stoking the furnaces by throwing endless shovels of coal through the furnace doors, black as the pit of hell, and choking with dust, and with the ship often heaving violently up and down, and from side to side. It was the most hellish job a man could do. And for little more than a pound a week. No wonder that industrial discontent was mounting in the years before the Great War.

If this was Dorothy's first chance to look around a big ship, it certainly wasn't to be her last; she was to have much closer contact with ships and everything associated with them in the years ahead, and I suspect that Jabez, when the time came, was not displeased to have a ship's officer as a son-in-law.

Nellie and I went to Miss Lambert's prize distribution and dance in the Central Hall, Pryme Street, on Friday Dec. 18th, 1908. The operetta 'Cinderella' was given by the pupils. Mrs. Larard gave the prizes, and Mrs. Lambert was presented with a gold pendant and chain, and Miss Williams with a silver serviette ring. Mrs. L. giving up the school.

Mrs. Lambert was indeed giving up the school. The *Hull Daily Mail* reported 'a touch of sadness when Mrs. Lambert referred to the fact that she was severing her connection with the Aston High School, of which she has been Principal for the past nine years. Miss Ferguson was to be her successor, and she congratulated the school on being so fortunate in having so qualified a lady to carry on the work.'

A delegation of former pupils later made a presentation to Mrs. Lambert at her Hornsea residence of a massive soup-tureen and bacon-dish combined, beautifully chased and inscribed 'Presented to Mrs. Lambert by former pupils of Aston High School, January 1909'. The donors, who included ex-pupils from England, Ireland, Italy and Germany, told Mrs.Lambert that no Principal was ever better loved and respected than the Principal of Aston High School.

One of Dorothy's old school chums, Muriel Middlebrook, won two of the school prizes that year. One of them was the German prize, a language at which she excelled, and it was through her that Dorothy made her German friends in Hull. Muriel worked in Germany up to the summer of 1914, and, when war broke out, put her linguistic ability to good use as an interpreter in the War Office.

Cricket on the sports field at Hymers College in 1910.

1909

Went with Doris and Elsie Ward to the matinee of 'The Dollar Princess' at the Grand, Saturday 27th Feb, '09. Kitty Gordon, Hilda Moody, Alice Pollard, Rob. Michaelis and Vernon Davidson principals.

The *Hull Daily Mail* had nothing but praise for *The Dollar Princess*:
'It is good in every sense and in every department. The plot is good. The music is better. The presentation is worthy of enconiums as high as anyone can bestow. *The Dollar Princess* is heralded as a sister piece with *The Merry Widow*. It has all the virtues of that vivacious work, but none of its failings. Among the musical pieces of its class, we do not recall anything which left so little room for reproach. It is original, it is diverting, it is ingenious. What more humorous than that an American millionaire, determined to get the most out of his dollars, should select his servants from the ranks of the English aristocracy. The idea is a delicious piece of satire. Why should a man like Phineas Q. Condor, President of the Oil Trust, hesitate to have his clothes brushed by a baron, and his dinner served by a duke, if he can get his titled people to accept his money, and a very pretty figure they cut. He has a daughter and a niece – and he wants to have a wife. If his lackey is a 'Sir', then his wife must be a Princess. And so they bring him from Russia a Princess Olga. Poor old Phineas. He falls in love with his princess, and she is no princess at all. But his millions have not spoilt him after all. Though the princess turns out to be a lion-tamer from the music halls, he marries her. Instead of a Princess he gets a Queen. His daughter pairs off with his secretary, and his niece takes a groom, who is an earl.

'The music of the piece is no trivial scoring but good composing, dignified in style, and often rising to the heights of real passion. This is far above the level of the sort of musical comedy we have had to listen to for the last ten years. George Edwardes has done something to be proud of in giving us a higher standard of music. It is high time somebody did.

'In the title role is no less charming and competent an artist than Miss Hilda Moody. With Mr. Robert Michaelis, who so admirably sings and acts as the millionaire's secretary, Miss Moody has some uncommonly fine scenes, and last night the love duets they sang were given with such force that the audience was moved to great enthusiasm. *The Dollar Princess* is staged on a lavish scale of splendour, and the dresses worn by the leading ladies will inspire unbounded enthusiasm and probably envy.'

After *The Dollar Princess* was first presented at Daly's in 1909, George Edwardes assembled the cast and told them, 'The show's too long – we must cut at least half an hour of the dialogue.' Willie Ward, a bit-player, piped up, 'I hope you won't cut any of mine, Guv'nor – I've only got one line – "Four Pounds, six shillings and ninepence." That's all I have got to say.' 'There you are,' said Edwardes solemnly, 'Make it eightpence-ha'penny' – We'll never get the curtain down.'

Went with Mother to the matinee of 'Butterflies', Saturday March 20th at the Grand.

Butterflies, with Ada Reeve, had been showing at the Apollo the previous year when Dorothy and her cousins had been in London; now, at long last, it had come to Hull for the week. It had enchanted Dorothy and her mother, especially the classical dance, *La Naissance du Papillon*, performed by Phyllis Monkman.

The *Hull Daily Mail* theatre critic called the play, 'The glorification of female sauciness. The phrase is not ours. It is from the lips of Mr. Christopher Podmore, one of the leading characters in *Butterflies*, and it happens to aptly describe the piece. *Butterflies* is frankest frivolity. The word "saucy" is singularly correct in application – "spicy" fits equally well. *Butterflies* is scarcely the kind of thing Mr. Forbes-Robertson would commend to the Dean of York as an example of the elevating tendency of the modern stage.

'The scene is set in Paris and we are among the students of art. Before the butterflies have been fluttering for two minutes the audience realises it is in the heart of Bohemia. Miss Ada Reeve, cast for the part of Rhodanthe the Witch, flashes through the play as the gayest of butterflies. Mercurial, volatile, piquant, daring, Miss Reeve is the central figure in the play. *Butterflies*, which is at the Grand Theatre, was received with cheers by a crowded house.'

Florrie left the Workhouse. I went to Hymers Sports with May Larard and Nellie with Muriel Middlebrook, May 1st 1909.

Florrie had once been the Dentons' housemaid, but Demon Drink the curse of the working class, had brought her to a sorry state, and she had found herself in the workhouse. A régime of hard work, plain food, and sound religious instruction had brought about a change in Florrie, and now she was out again to face the world. The Sculcoates Union Workhouse on Beverley Road was a grim institution, a place to be feared as much as the House of Correction and the Lunatic Asylum. It was where so many of the destitute or chronically ill ended their days.

The *Hull Daily Mail* in the early years of the century was a rich source of stories about the workhouse and its inmates, especially around 1909 when a Royal Commission on the Poor Law had just reported. The Commission had recommended that the young, the aged, the sick, and the mentally feeble, should no longer be lumped together in the public wards, and that the work-shy should be despatched to the House of Correction. There was a good deal less sensitivity in Edwardian times towards the unfortunate inmates of these institutions, and they were frequently the objects of cruel humour. Music-hall comedians often made them the butt of their 'jokes' and there was at the time popular recitation which began, '*It was Christmas Day in the Workhouse . . .*' and ended with the inmates telling the Workhouse Master what to do with his Christmas pudding. But the following account in the *Bridlington Free Press* was written as a straight piece of reporting. Under the somewhat depressing heading of CHRISTMAS IN THE WORKHOUSE, the correspondent wrote: 'The day will live long in the memory of those who occupy the "home" which is known as the Workhouse. The dining room was delightfully decorated with evergreens and coloured paper and mottoes and lanterns, and there were two Christmas trees in place. There are more occupants in the Bridlington workhouse than there have been for thirty or forty years, and the best use was made of all available space. The dining room with its ancient tables and white scrubbed forms is not a very attractive place on ordinary days, but on Friday it was almost worthy of the title of a banqueting hall. It was cosy and comfortable, and a very pleasant couple of hours was spent in it.

'The fare consisted of roast beef and roast pork, gravies, potatoes and turnips, and, as usual, the roast pork was the favourite joint. It was not on the ordinary dietary of the year, and so at Christmastide it comes as something of a novelty, and those who care for the old folks know how dear to their old gums is a piece of well-browned "crackling". When the *entrées* had been done full justice to, the plum puddings came on. Such puddings of such size and such quality, and the sauce, and rum sauce too, seemed as much enjoyed as the puddings themselves. The fruits were on the decorated table; the apples and oranges the guests as a rule put in their pockets for another occasion.

'Those who could not leave the wards, including the patients in the infirmary, were looked after there, being served first in their own place, and the children, of whom at present there are an unusually large number, were dined in the kitchen and had a very happy time.'

'A generous firm of brewers sent a cask of beer, so that those who like a glass of ale were at liberty to have it. This part of the business was under the personal supervision of the Master, and it need hardly be said that, as in former years, it was dealt out with great discrimination. There was an ample supply of lemonade, and perhaps hop-bitters, for those who do not care for intoxicants.'

But some of the inmates of the workhouse must have sorely tried the patience of the long-suffering staff, as in this case reported in the *Hull Daily Mail*:

'Mr. Jones, the aged hero of a gruesome practical joke, was ordered by the Board of Guardians to leave the workhouse. Jones had proved such an unmanageable inmate that he was incarcerated in the workhouse mortuary with the body of a dead pauper. Nothing daunted, he removed the corpse from the coffin, propped the body against the wall, and took his place.

'When a maid servant entered the chamber shortly afterwards with food, she was transfixed by the ghastly sight. From the coffin came an unearthly voice which said, "If he can't eat it, I can." The terrified girl fainted away. Threatened yesterday with legal proceedings unless he departed, Jones coolly replied, "I might as well be in prison as any other home."'

House painted outside June 1909.

What ever his abilities as an accountant may have been, Jabez was not a do-it-yourself enthusiast. Few men were in those days. It would have been almost unheard of for a middle-class house-owner to paint his own house with labour so cheap, and in any case, he would have considered it is his duty, 'to give employment to the artisan'. A first-class tradesman charged no more than sevenpence an hour for his labour, and a pint pot of paint cost about eightpence. With burning-off and making-good, priming, undercoating and with two coats of gloss paint, a house the size of Oban Villa would have have taken a good man about three weeks to paint outside, and he would have charged Jabez no more than £20. Today it would cost well over a £1,000, a sum which in Jabez's day would have bought him a splendid house in the country.

Economic comparisons between then and now are fairly pointless, but in an age when the £ is worth the merest fraction of its 1909 value, it is salutary to ponder over a small paragraph in the *Hull Daily Mail* of 6 March, 1909, headed 'WHAT A FARTHING WILL BUY' – 'A big farthing trade is done in many small shops in Hull's poorer quarters. The farthing will buy any of the following articles: a quarter-ounce of tea, 1½ ounces of sugar, half a quarter of a pint of milk, and the same of vinegar; four small biscuits, a small piece of salt, a teaspoonful of pepper, and the same of mustard: a tablespoonful of rice or pearl-barley, or an onion. Of other necessities, a farthing will likewise purchase a knob of blue, a small number of pins, needles, or hair-grips, a bodkin, a skein of thread or wool.'

For the benefit of younger readers, a farthing was a quarter of an old penny, and if it still existed today would be worth roughly one-thousandth part of £1.

On my birthday received a gold pendant and chain from Father. Had May to tea. Tom left same day for London on his bicycle.

Hull to London was a long way to ride on a bicycle, at least 240 miles, and cycles in 1909 were not the light-weight, multi-geared machines they are today. And the tyres were by no means as tough; they were particularly vulnerable to sharp stones and discarded horse-shoe nails. If Tom had less than six punctures on his ride to London I should be very surprised.

The roads in town and country alike were peaceful and safe for those who used them. The country towns were small and clearly defined, with no urban sprawl, and the fields and hedgerows stretched away for mile after mile. It probably took Tom two, or even three days, to reach London, finding his bed overnight at village inns, or at farm houses along the Great North Road, the road that the stage-coaches and pack-horses before him had followed for centuries. Or perhaps he wheeled his bike on to the Humber ferry and cycled down from New Holland through the little-used roads and lanes of Lincolnshire and Eastern England. Whichever way he went, the ride was a real test of his stamina.

Thomas Wreghitt Andrews was 18-years-old that summer; he was a Hull Grammar School boy, the son of an architect living in Malm Street off the Boulevard, and his sister, Joan, was a school-friend of Dorothy's. It was Tommy Andrews who had given her the autograph book, and she makes frequent mention of him in her diary. The previous summer she had noted that he had left for a holiday in Terneuzen in Holland, and perhaps she envied him the opportunity to travel abroad.

Shortly after he returned from London Tom was attending the annual Territorial Camp in Lincolnshire. He was typical of the better-educated patriotic type of boy who became a voluntary part-time soldier, and in

1914 it was on boys like Tommy Andrews that England had to rely until it could mobilise its full strength.

Hospital Saturday June 26th. Helped at Mayoress's stand and then went to Feldmans for tea.

Dorothy had been pressed into helping collect for 'Hospital Saturday' by Becci Feldman, the Mayor's daughter. Both Becci Feldman and May Larard, daughter of the previous Mayor, were schoolfriends of Dorothy.

The Mayoress and her helpers had worked hard on a wet Saturday to raise money for the local hospitals., their efforts being reported in the *Hull Daily Mail*, and this year they had published a picture of the helpers on the streets. Press photographs were relatively rare in 1909, the photographic plates being expensive to produce:

'The ladies did bravely in the cause of charity at Hull under most depressing circumstances. As a result of their persistency, £426.14.10 (and a farthing) was collected on behalf of the hospitals. The ladies were very businesslike, and when "I have already given" was the answer, the retort was generally, "Only another copper, please." The Mayoress, (Mrs. Feldman) was the centre of a very busy scene at the Bridge, arriving about eight o-clock. The Sheriff (Dr. Gautby) was also early astir to catch the early coppers, and the Mayor was frequently observed in the vicinity.

'At the Mayoress's stand there were Mrs. Norman, Mrs. Gore, Mrs. Forty, Mrs. McCombe, the Misses Kelsey, Forty, Tether, B. Feldman, M. Feldman, Master H. Feldman, Mrs. Aaron, Mrs. Jarman, Mrs. Nettleton, Miss Darby, Miss Denton, Miss Johnson and Miss Larard.

'During the afternoon the Hull City Police Band played on Monument Bridge, and there were also three processions in the side streets, the idea being that nobody should escape. There was, it is understood, a tacit agreement that the fair collectors should be permitted to collect on the cars, having to remain on them until a stopping place was reached, but in some cases they were asked for their fares.

'The counting was completed at a midnight meeting in the Outpatients' Dept. at the Infirmary. The result was received with gratification, and the collectors heartily thanked, as were the band, the proprietors of the theatres and music-halls for allowing collection, the Hull City Garage for the loan of a car, and others.'

Went with Father to the opening of the cricket match, Yorks/Lancs v Australia on Thursday July 29th, 1909.

Even though Hull was Yorkshire's third largest city, it got less than a fair share of first-class cricket. Leeds and Sheffield and Bradford hogged most of the county fixtures, and Scarborough had its two-week Cricket Festival each September, but this year the public of Hull were to be compensated by a visit from the Australian touring side playing a combined Yorkshire and Lancashire team at the Circle. What a pity the weather didn't live up to the occasion – the summer of 1909 was a typically wet one.

The Circle cricket ground, home of Hull C.C., could hardly have been more convenient for the Dentons; adjacent to the West Park, it was barely five minutes walk from their house on Anlaby Road. On one side of the cricket ground stood the barn-like stand of Hull City Football Club, and on another the greens of Hull Bowling Club, and here Jabez, a member of both clubs, had his seat. Behind the Circle the Railway Clerks played on an odd-shaped piece of ground, where, if I remember rightly, a hit to the boundary counted for only two runs. While County members enjoyed the comfort of seats on the pavilion with back-rests, the ordinary spectators had to sit on rows of benches, exposed to the elements – the 'six-penny' customer received scant consideration at any sporting event in Edwardian days. If it rained he would have to try and get into the beer tent which the Hull Brewery always erected for the County games.

Jabez and Dorothy enjoyed a good day's cricket on the Thursday, despite interruptions caused by the rain. The *Hull Daily Mail* reported:

'On Tuesday the wicket was under water and this morning very soft. The attendance was below expectations at around 3,000, due to fears of more rain. But the sun broke through after lunch and the turnstiles clicked with a regularity to delight the heart of the treasurer. At lunch the receipts were £150.

Yorks/Lancs batted first and the score at the end of the first day's play read:

Spooner c McCartney b Cotter	66
Hartley b McCartney	11
Denton c Whitty b O'Connor	55
Tyldersley b O'Connor	8
Rhodes not out	75
Makepeace not out	29
Extras	17
Total (for 4 wickets)	261

But on the following day the sports writer, with little cricket to describe, wrote about the free lunch the club had stood him:

'Hull Cricket Club have entertained the Press quite royally, for which I offer best thanks. During lunch Mr. Langley Morris of the Gramophone Supply Co. gave some excellent records on the gramophone... play was held up at one stage while a boy's kite was removed from the ground... and then it came on to rain. Those who had been fortunate enough to bring umbrellas stuck to their seats, but less fortunate individuals made a rush for whatever cover they could find, although a fair number, with no protection save straw hats, braved the elements.'

Unfortunately for these optimists, the rain did not relent, and the second and third days' play were abandoned. Among the disappointed spectators at the Circle that day were a nine-year-old Teddie Denton and his young friend, Rex Alston. Rex, who was later to become the well-known B.B.C. cricket commentator, lived near the Dentons – his father Rev. Arthur F. Alston, was the vicar of St. Matthew's Church on the Boulevard.

On Saturday August 6th Mother, Father and I went to a Military Tournament on the Football Ground given by the 5th 2nd Lancers from York. Enjoyed it immensely.

The *Hull Daily Mail*, as usual, provided the detail missing in Dorothy's brief entry in her diary:

'Those fine soldiers of the 5th Irish Lancers made a welcome appearance in the city and during the afternoon provided the first of three brilliant performances at the Hull F.C. ground at the Boulevard. The crowd who witnessed three and a half hours of a most interesting display of horsemanship, and a grand exhibition of the finer points of cavalry work, were delighted with the performance, and were unanimous in their views that the military tournament, an innovation for Hull, should be repeated every year.'

'So varied were the items in yesterday's display, and so exacting were they, that there was never a dull moment in the afternoon's sport. "Wonderful indeed", and "extremely clever" are statements befitting the display of these fine fellows in their regimental dress of red and blue. As for the spirited horses, one cannot fail to be impressed with their smartness and the thorough understanding they show in every movement they are required to perform.'

'Misfortunes never come singly at the Hull Skating Rink.'

Vesta Tilley: music hall star famous for male impersonations.

William Jackson and Son Ltd., grocers, 1906.

'The programme of cantering and jumping and formation riding included "slicing the lemon", cutting the suspended fruit in half with their swords, and picking up tent pegs stuck in the ground with points of their lances while at full gallop; there was "wrestling on horseback", musical rides, and a push-ball match, and a well-trained horse dribbled a ball the length of the field, and "scored a goal" to loud applause.'

On Monday afternoon October 18th went to the opening of the Trades Exhibition, and at night went to the opening of the Newington Rink by Mayor Feldman.

Roller-skating was the newest craze of the Edwardian era which the *Hull Daily Mail* reported under the headline – 'ROLLER SKATING – HULL TAKES TO THE PASTIME':

'At 7 o-clock promptly the scarlet-coated band, which will play daily, rendered *God Save the King*. There was a clamour to get on the Samuel Winslow skates, and in a few minutes the rinking had commenced. It was surprising how everybody at once seemed to tumble to the idea.

'With the exercise of a little common sense it seemed one can instinctively take to the rollers. People of course always catch on to a new thing, but judging from the expressions used, roller-skating, or rinking, has this time come to stay. It was surprising how few bumps there were, and, what there were, constituted the sole price for acquiring a new method of progression, and could not be regarded as in any way excessive.

'When there was a tumble, and it was by no means always the ladies, down swooped one of the instructors in plum-coloured suits, to raise the fallen, and then skimmed back to the centre. It was interesting to watch these instructors skimming round and round the rink, backwards as a rule, watching the skating and circling around, and ready in a twinkling to be of assistance to anybody in need.

'An outstanding trim figure in a green costume was particularly graceful, and the admiration of rinkers as she turned and whirled with a sudden variety of direction, that is with the power of a bird. Roller-skating is described as most nearly approaching the motions of a flying bird. It was remarked to this clever rinker that there were many young ladies in Hull just longing to rink like her. Miss Sturgeon, for that is her name, replied that it was quite easy, and splendid exercise for very little effort. You just start off walking. Girls who dance can usually rink well. Miss Sturgeon is connected with the rink and her skill comes from experience of many rinks.'

'There will be three sessions a day, the admission for ladies in the evenings being sixpence, with a shilling for the skates. Refreshments are provided with the music, and the rink should prove a popular meeting place in Hull.'

But the new craze did not please everybody. The 'Letters' column of the *Hull Daily Mail* carried this complaint:

'Sir,

There is no doubt that rinking has had a serious effect on trade, especially on the retail shopkeeper, and there are hundreds who go rinking who cannot afford it. I maintain that rinking carried to excess is not only bad for trade, but dangerous to us as a people, and lowering the moral standards of the nation. Why? Because there are people who do not care how they get the money, but get it they must, and they do. For instance, a young lady goes to her grocer getting a quantity of goods on credit, and immediately goes and sells them for half the cost of each for cash, so that she may go rinking. A young girl employed behind the counter was continuously going rinking; her employer knew that, even if her parents let her keep all her wages, they would not pay for the expenses of the same, and reluctantly had to come to one conclusion, with one result.'

'Fathers and Mothers, think twice before allowing your sons and daughters to commence this craze, for, no doubt, it is a craze, and a most alluring one – and thereby hope to keep them from falling morally, if not physically injuring themselves. To my knowledge, there have been cases of injured spines, fractured ankles and several fractured wrists. In conclusion, I would urge all shopkeepers to raise a strong protest against any further music licences being granted, and also that our worthy mayor will refrain from opening, or being present at any future opening of such.'

Went to see England v Sweden at football Saturday 6th Nov. 1909. England won 7 - 0.

Top-class football had only come to Hull in 1904 with the founding of Hull City F.C. and the opening of the Anlaby Road ground. Soccer soon found its supporters in Hull, as it did in all the large Northern and Midland cities. The playing of an international match at Anlaby Road was considered an honour for the City and the *Hull Daily Mail* reported:

'The first international match on the banks of the Humber was Hull's distinction this afternoon. It had been devoutedly desired for a long time past. The Swedish players had the opportunity of getting into trim on the

Hull City ground, having been in the City for several days. They were joined at the Royal Station Hotel on Friday evening by the English amateurs, who arrived in two's and three's from various parts of the country.

'The Swedish players have not a great command of the English language, but it was a practical *entente cordiale* to see them all sitting down to lunch. Vivian Woodward was in command of the English forces, and his side included our own Gordon Wright, and, among others, Herbert Smith, formerly of Hull City and Reading fame, whom some consider a "one-legged" back, but a good one at that. As for Sweden, they did not physically suggest lambs going to the slaughter, but it was a compliment to put such an English side against them.

'England's team – R.G. Brebner (Darlington), W.S. Corbett (Birmingham), H. Smith (Reading), W. Faye (St. Albans), F.W. Chapman (South Nottingham), W. Olley (Clapton), A. Berry (Fulham), V.J. Woodward (Chelmsford), H. Stapley (Glossop), A.S. Owen (Leicester Fosse), and K.G.D. Wright (Hull City).

'Referee: Mr. J. Groothoff.

'There would be an attendance of about 7,000 when Woodward led out the English side in their white shirts. Reserved benches on the stand were occupied by well known personages of the football world, such as Mr. Clegg, Chairman of the Football Association, and Mr. Wall, its statesmanlike secretary, while the East Riding County F.A. and the Lincs County F.A. had their heads in Mr. Alf Spring and Mr. Bellamy of Grimsby. The spin of the coin was a victory for England . . .', and so eventually was the match, which England won 7-0.

The *Mail* commented: 'It is so very different in football in which there are no league points at the end of it. The two countries showed what is known as "gentlemanly football". We can do with some of it in Hull where we have been watching the game long enough to appreciate it from an exhibition point of view. Someone whispers that we should get it in the First Division' – (a whisper which has must surely have faded away after 90 years of striving and hoping) – 'The game was so one-sided as to be an exposition of doubtful quality. The Swedes are much better at skiing.'

A rather unkind dig at the Swedes who were then, like most of the Continentals, mere tyros at a game which the British had invented. But the amateur game, which had been developed by the Public Schools in the Victorian era, was now becoming dominated by the professional, to the disgust of many. The social distinction between the amateur and the professional could not have been more marked. Christopher Martin in his book *The Edwardians* writes:

Football action in the early years of the Century.

On winding country roads a man could cycle in perfect safety - but they were hell on the tyres.

'In contrast with the rough Northern and Midland footballers were the graceful amateur Corinthians. They seemed to personify in their dashing, dilettante brilliance, the gay gallantry which the Great War pillaged. Simply to see them saunter on to a football field, scorning shin-pads, in their fresh white cricket shirts, was to feel the difference between their patrician negligence and the professional footballers of the industrial towns.'

In *Association Football and the Men who Made it*, William Pickford went further when he wrote: 'The professional footballer has degraded the pastime. For many of the troublesome offshoots of the revolutionary act of 1885 (the legalisation of professionalism), the misguided enthusiasm of the hard-working toilers in the big cities has been to blame. The professional has always played to orders given to him, and moulded his conduct and methods on those of his superiors. When he has been wisely controlled and guided he has proved the best of fellows. But many of the professional players are of small moral fibre and cannot be expected to possess a very high standard of ethics.'

Of Vivian Woodward, England's captain in the match at Hull, he wrote: 'He is easily recognised in a crowd . . . he has a pleasant face to look upon. To a clear complexion are added a firm mouth, strongly marked eyebrows, and a keen clear eye that can take in a situation at a glance. One could not mistake him for other than an amateur.'

Went to 'A Waltz Dream' at the Grand with Tottie on Saturday Nov. 27th. Robert Evett as Nikki; Maudie Thornton, Amy Augarde etc.

'Those people who filled the Grand Theatre on Monday received the pleasurable tremor for which we believe they paid their money', writes the *Hull Daily Mail*. 'It is well known that the slimmest of plots is built around – and is partially an excuse for – a kiss episode, and a waltz, cunningly turned and varied. If much of the fun-making in *A Waltz Dream* is obvious, at least there is no attempt to conceal its obviousness. In fact this quality is insisted on as one of the charms of the piece which, it is fair to say, has many others.

'That alluring and frolicsome Viennese refrain is the main one, however. Capital solo singing and deft dancing supplement it. Would that we could say half as much in praise of the libretto. There are no trailing lengths of weariness – the dialogue is too good humoured for that, but there are patches of frivolous patter that any drawing room circle could improvise just as well.

'A delightful feature is the ladies' orchestra, among whom too there are several unusually clever dancers, who gaily footed it around the bandstand in a genuinely bright scene. Musically it may be a paradox, yet it is a fact that the fascination exercised by modern sensuous values – and there are a whole phalanx of them beside *The Merry Widow* – is derived from a distinctly *cantabile* treatment of the tune.

'A personal triumph is won by Robert Evett as Lieut. Nikki. It was his first appearance in Hull, and the impression he created was unmistakable – to get to our good graces was the work of a few minutes . . . in brief, *The Waltz Dream* was highly enjoyed by a large Hull audience.'

Anlaby Road, Hull: the building with the flagstaff is the Palace Theatre.

Saturday Market, Beverley, 1910, without a vehicle in sight.

A scene of rural tranquillity early in the Century: the village of Anlaby.

1910

Joan came to tea January 5th. Ted and I went to Bridlington on 6th January 1910, and came home on the 19th. Gertie and Doris there also. Went to the Rink, the Pictures and Grantham's Panto. Gertie met David Palmer. Had a lovely time.

Winter in Bridlington. It had been a hard winter too. The *Bridlington Free Press* reported that in the week before Christmas there had been 22 degrees of frost, even though by Christmas Day a south-east wind had brought a gradual thaw. But residents and visitors had had their full share of seasonal entertainment that Christmas. At the Spa Grantham's Juvenile Pantomime Company put on *Sinbad the Sailor*, an amateur production to raise money for charity, and there was an orchestra playing on the Parade. And now Bridlington had its own roller-skating rink and its Animated Picture Palace. But often on a winter's evening, when the wind was howling around the chimney pots and the rain beating on the window panes, it was cosy to sit around the fireside and listen to Grandma Dobson telling the children the familiar story of the Great Bridlington Storm of 1871, in which Grandpa Dobson and his fellow townsmen had played such a stalwart role. In that year the Dobsons had lived above the saddler's shop in King Street: Kate was a girl of 11, and Clara and Jinny very young schoolgirls.

On 9 February, 1871, about 400 ships, which had been waiting in Northern ports for a favourable wind, left their berth in mild and genial weather, with a moderate north-west wind behind them, heading down the East Coast. On the Thursday afternoon many people gathered along the coast to watch the stirring sight of this fleet of southbound vessels. During the evening, however, the wind dropped and many of the ships with their cargoes of coal, were becalmed in Bridlington Bay. But during the night the wind picked up again, veered about, and suddenly a tempestuous storm arose, increasing to hurricane force. The fleet of ships now found themselves on a lee shore in the teeth of a south-easterly gale.

As day broke the masters of some of the vessels made a run for the harbour, whilst others, which had tried to ride out the storm, were driven, helplessly dragging their anchors, towards the shore. Robert Dobson and many of the local tradesmen locked up their shops and gathered near the harbour, peering out to sea through the blinding snow as the full force of the storm broke over Bridlington Bay. Both of the town's lifeboats and the rocket apparatus had been made ready for use since first light. The first vessel in distress was a sailing brig which tried to run for shelter, but missed the harbour mouth and splintered to pieces against the sea wall. Rocket attempts failed to get a line aboard her, and the lifeboat had to go out and bring the crew to safety. At mid-morning five more vessels were driven ashore under the sea-wall, and again the two lifeboats went to their aid bringing the crews ashore – the *Harbinger* picked up over 20 men. A collier was driven aground below Sewerby and, as the crew jumped into the angry sea, the local men waded out to their armpits and dragged them to safety. Meanwhile, Anna Dobson and Kate were helping the local women to prepare food and hot drinks and dry clothing for the men.

By noon the lifeboat crews were exhausted, their hands raw and bleeding, but many vessels were still in great danger. The *Harbinger* with a makeshift crew, went out to the brig *Delta* of Whitby, which was ashore to the south of the harbour; four of the crew attempted to get off in their own boat, but were swamped by a huge wave and all four were swept away and lost. Then the lifeboat crew saw that the captain of the brig was clinging to his doomed vessel and worked the boat into a position to take him off – but at the very moment when the coxwain called to the man to jump, a wave rising with terrific force plunged the lifeboat, end-foremost, into the boiling waters. The nine men of the crew were pitched into the sea, struggling for their lives; the boat quickly righted itself, and three of the crew, who had clung to the ropes on her side, were swept back into the lifeboat. They drifted helplessly in the storm, without oars or means of navigation, until the lifeboat was washed ashore on the south side of Bridlington. But the other six brave men of the crew perished, tragically within sight of their families and friends who were powerless to help them. The six who lost their lives were well known and respected men of the town.

All that afternoon the terrible storm continued. The brig *Produce* of Folkstone struck close to the north side of the pier. Boats were lowered and the crew got in, but were swamped before leaving the vessel's side; two of the men attempted to swim for the pier, watched by a crowd who, though almost within arm's length, could render them no assistance; they watched, frantic at their own impotence, as the men were swept beneath the waves. Four other men on the ship held on for grim life to the rigging, clinging for four hours with numbed hands, crying for help that could never come. At four o-clock, on the high tide, the vessel lurched shoreward and turned over, and the men disappeared for ever. Women and children shrieked; men, strong and stalwart, wept.

But the work of destruction and loss of life was not yet complete. In the growing dark a man was seen waving a light on the foreyard of a schooner near to the pier. Repeatedly a line was fired by rocket from the shore, women and children grasping the line to pull it in each time it failed, but to no avail. Another man could be seen by the light of a gaslamp on the pier, clinging to a piece of the wreck, but no one could help him, and he too, with the remainder of the crew, was lost from sight. All that day the people of Bridlington, men, women and children, worked without rest in their attempts to rescue men from the clutches of a cruel sea.

Out at sea signals of distress were seen all night as two more vessels were lost off Flamborough Head. The night was the most dreadful ever known on the north-east coast of England. During that Friday night Robert Dobson and many more people of the town never left the beach or the pier. As the tide went down and the storm abated, the full scale of the disaster was revealed. Parts of ship's hulls, entangled spars, beams, sails, wood, coal, anchors, chains and ropes littered the shore – here and there a sou'wester, a solitary boot, a torn chart. And the sea gave up its dead. As well as the six brave men of the Bridlington lifeboat, a further 25 bodies were washed ashore, some of them never to be identified.

On Tuesday 14 February, 1871, the quiet churchyard of Bridlington Priory received 23 of the drowned sailors, and over the next few days 20 more were laid to rest beside them. Altogether it was reckoned that 70 men and 30 ships were lost in Bridlington Bay on the fateful 10 February, 1871. The Great Storm was a catastrophe that people of Grandma Dobson's generation never forgot. Those who worked so gallantly to save and succour lives each received a letter of thanks from Count Bathyany, a wealthy benefactor of the town, who had provided one of the lifeboats. Grandma Dobson treasured the letter and kept it in the the drawer of her writing-desk; I remember seeing it as a small boy, but what happened to it I have often wondered – I expect, like so many irreplaceable relics of the past, it ended up in the dustbin. The three surviving members of the ill-fated crew of the *Harbinger* published a letter in the local press expressing 'their heartfelt thanks to Mr. Robert Dobson who, with others, rendered such timely assistance to them when they drifted on to the south beach, without means to help themselves, their physical energies being exhausted, and conveying them to a place of safety.'

Went with Tottie to 'Our Miss Gibbs' Feb. 25th 1910. Blanche Brown as Mary Gibbs, George Gregory as Jim Gibbs – wonderful dresses – simply grand!

Our Miss Gibbs was another of George Edwarde's highly successful musical comedies. Set in Garrod's Store and the Court of Honour at the

Franco-British Exhibition in Paris, it featured bevies of beautifully dressed girls, the fabulous *Edwardian Belles* and the handsome young dudes.

The stylish and elegant fashion of the Edwardian age has never been surpassed, and the Grand Theatre audience gasped with appreciation as the curtain rose on the second act on these gorgeous creatures, with their 'hour-glass' figures, draped in gowns of breath-taking elegance, and adorned with fabulous picture hats – each girl was reputed to carry 60 guineas-worth of millinery on her head. *Our Miss Gibbs* was a show that had everything, a good plot, brilliant costumes, artistic settings, melodious tunes, singing, dancing and humour. As Dorothy said – it was simply grand!

Nellie and I went to hear the new King proclaimed on Tuesday May 10th, 1910.

King Edward VII's short reign was over. Already a middle-aged man when he came to the throne on the death of Queen Victoria in 1901, he was not destined to rule for long. The passing of the monarch was marked with all pomp and circumstance, but in 1910 the King was still a remote figure to most ordinary people.

Kate Dobson told an unlikely tale of walking alone on the North Pier at Bridlington late one summer evening when a portly gentleman raised his hat to her and wished her 'good evening'. She always maintained that it was Edward, the Prince of Wales, but the family treated her claim with scepticism and maintained that it was it was an Edward VII look-alike with a roving eye for the ladies.

The *Hull Daily Mail* reported the ceremony at the City Hall with all the editorial verbosity at its command:

'The proclamation of King George V took place in Hull this noon with all due solemnity befitting the occasion. North, South, East and West, from Simla to Cape Town, from Brisbane to Gibraltar, from Khartoum to British Honduras, King George V was proclaimed ruler over a quarter of the globe which lives in British peace.

'Everyone who witnessed the solemn act felt that he or she was a child of the new era . . . Then forward, the shrine shines bright before us – England's high destiny. Around us the drums roll, the kingly clarion call. Let us raise our eyes to the bright goal, and our souls to the occasion. With united hearts and voices let us proclaim our deathless love and service!

GOD SAVE THE KING.'

Uncle Harry died May 24th. Buried May 26th.

Like his father before him, Harry Fenner died in the prime of his life. He was only 45, and his death came as a great shock to all the family. Three generations of Fenners died before their time. In 1886 Joseph Fenner, the founder of the family firm making leather machine belting, was killed in a road accident when he was thrown from his trap on a sharp bend on a country lane – (it is said that the 50-year-old Joe was driving furiously to show off to his mistress at the time) – his son Harry died suddenly in his 40's, and Jack, Harry's eldest son, was killed with the East Yorkshire Regiment in France in 1917.

The *Hull Daily Mail* reported 'more than a touch of pathos in the funeral of Mr H.J. Fenner, whose death took place at Hornsea. The sadness was that Mr Fenner died away from home while spending a Bank Holiday weekend at the seaside.' His death was reported to have taken place 'after a short and painful illness'. He had a stomach ulcer, but he apparently ignored medical advice and insisted on driving his own horse and trap to Hornsea on Whit Monday. He collapsed in great pain on the way there and died before a doctor could reach him.

Harry Fenner was the joint Managing Director with his brother of the successful firm of J.H. Fenner & Co. of Marfleet; he was President of the Hull Conservative Union and a leading Freemason. His funeral was a big affair, attended by all the Denton family except Dorothy and Nellie (assuming the reporter to have got his facts right). The Press listed the mourners by name, adding at the end 'and two maids at Anlaby Road', who presumably did not have names.

The report concluded; 'A sad incident is that the eldest daughter was to have been married in a few days time, and only on Sunday the banns were called for the second time' However, cousin Elsie married Percy Barugh on 8 June, 1910, at St. Matthew's Church in the Boulevard, more or less as planned. And Aunt Jinne herself remarried a few years later.

Grannie died on June 14th, 1910.. Had a stroke on 11th and was buried on June 17th.

Grannie Dobson was an old lady of nearly 80. She had known hard times in her early years of marriage, but had outlived Robert Dobson by almost 20 years. They said the sudden death of her son-in-law, Harry Fenner, three weeks before, had upset her, and hastened her end. Old age was a state to be dreaded by millions of widows, but Grandma Dobson had been fortunate – she had her own house and an unmarried daughter to look after her. The previous year the Liberal Government had introduced Old Age Pensions, but a patronising, (and inaccurate) article in the *Bridlington Free Press* must have made Anna Dobson profoundly thankful that she had not had to depend on the State for help in her own old age:

'One of our representatives had a conversation with an old lady who had just put into her dilapidated purse the two half-crowns she had received under the Government Old Age Pensions Act. She said she was very proud to have lived to see this day, and, to her surprise, had been told in the Post Office that she had to go every week for her five shillings as long as she lived – she had thought they would only be paid out occasionally.

She became very confidential and spoke of the immense joy five shillings a week would bring to her life, and the lives of those connected with her. She was going to spend a part of the first shilling on the purchase of a mutton chop, and this was the greatest luxury she could fancy. She lived with her son-in-law, who was very kind to her, and had told her that morning to purchase whatever little dainty she fancied with her own money. She had wanted for nothing the years she had lived with her son-in-law and her daughter, but they were hard working people with a small income, and she had a fear that she was taking from their little store what they required for themselves and their children. Now, however, by keeping herself, there would be added joy in the home, and she anticipated that she would now and then be able to have a chop and a rice pudding and that sort of thing.

A feature of *Silver Friday* was the assistance given to the old folks by the Post Office officials, who showed the courtesy and kindness which is characteristic of them. One official spoke of the peculiar pleasure it afforded to see at least one couple march off hand in hand with ten shillings* between them. The gratitude of all the pensioners had been pleasing and touching to witness.'

*(a married couple in fact received only 7/6d. a week)

I stayed at Bridlington until July 13th. 'Vagabonds' and 'Smart Set' on Parade. 'Gay Birds' and Annie Croft on the Spa.

This was the hey-day of the pierrots and the seaside concert parties. On the North Side sands a crowd began to gather, and the *Hull Daily Mail's* 'Gossiping Commissioner' wrote:

'No need to wonder twice what the crowd may mean. The Pierrots are coming out of course. Be sure that where ever there are Pierrots there will be a crowd. Beloved Pierrots. Pierrots adored of simple maidens. The Pierrots, glory of the twentieth century. Where are ye now, ye Nigger Minstrels? Came ye unto these yellow sands? Think ye your sable faces and carmine lips and woolly wigs would draw a crowd around? Write Ichabod, Messrs Nigger Minstrels, for your glory has departed and the Pierrots are in your place. Listen to the laughter ye old entertainers. Mark the rapt attention of the girls as the gentlemen in white raiment sing their songs of love and longing.'

The Pierrots, who performed in the open air, had to brave the elements of the English climate, but in the summer of 1910 there was, at Bridlington's Grand Pavilion, a full season of that modern form of indoor entertainment, the seaside concert party. It began in April with *The Nonentities* and was followed by *The Dandies*, who, according to the *Bridlington Free Press*, had the honour of appearing at Sandringham by Royal Command. Then came old Brid favourites, Harold Montague and his *Vagabonds*, increased that year to eight in number.

The chief attraction of the summer was *The Smart Set*, a party considered only second to Mr. Pelliser's *Follies*, and they were booked for several weeks; they were followed by Mr. Phillip Brahms's *March Hares*, including Mr. David Burnaby, the celebrated humourist. Later in the summer came Mr. D'Arcy's well-known company, *The Gipsies and the Jester*, and the season concluded with Mr. Stewart Alexander's *So-and-So's*. In addition, the Royal Dominion Animated Picture Company gave 'delightful examples of animated photography twice daily during the season.'

Annie Croft, who appeared at the Spa, was a talented Hull girl who sang and danced, and whose origins were attributed by unkind gossips to a liaison between a Society beauty and King Edward VII – hence Croft, as in Tranby Croft. There must have been any number of Annie Crofts throughout the realm if King Teddie's reputation is to be believed.

Mother and I went to spend the afternoon at Cold Harbour on August 16th, 1910. Charles met us and drove us around Molescroft to Bishop Burton. Had tea, played tennis. Then Massey and Chas drove us to the station.

Charles Denton, Dorothy's 18-year-old brother, left Hymers in 1908 and became a pupil farmer at John Dunning's Cold Harbour Farm at Bishop Burton. Two years younger than his sister, Charles was different in personality and outlook from Dorothy and the other Denton children – less outgoing, and, at times, taciturn of manner. All his life he was a man who preferred an outdoor life to an office desk, and farming suited him well.

On that August afternoon in 1910 Charles met his mother and sister with the farm run-about at Beverley railway station, and drove them the four miles to Cold Harbour farm – an enjoyable drive for the ladies through the old market town. Saturday Market was, as always on market days, buzzing with activity, the pavements crowded with townsmen and village folk who had come in from the East Riding villages to shop.

Beverley in 1910 was one of the gems of England's small country towns, graced by the twin towers of its mediaeval Minster, surely one of the most impressive churches in Europe, and its equally beautiful mediaeval church of St. Mary at the north end of the town. The stately Georgian houses beyond the North Bar were once the homes of wealthy residents, and now, many of them, mellowing with age, had become the offices of country solicitors and auctioneers: the shop windows of Briggs and Powell, offering the farming community a range of agricultural wares, held the attention of a group of farming men who had just emerged from the Beverley Arms, the town's best-known hostelry. Like the rest of the pubs, of which Beverley had a great many, it had been open since before breakfast time.

Charles held the reins loosely as the old horse, making its own way back to the farm, negotiated the narrow gap through the 15th-century brickwork of the North Bar and headed up the gravel driveway of New Walk, shaded by rows of leafy chestnuts, its leisurely pace giving Dorothy and her mother opportunity to examine and comment on the comfortable homes of Beverley's well-to-do. At the other end of New Walk they were into the village of Molescroft.

It was harvest time and in the fields around Molescroft the labours of reaping, binding and stooking were following their seasonal pattern. The hedgerows promised an abundance of brambles, and the pink and white dog roses, meadow-sweet and willow herb spread unchecked on the verges by the roadside. In the cottage gardens the laden branches of the apple trees were beginning to bend beneath the weight of fruit. As they drove along the lanes, languid and drowsy in the afternoon heat, Dorothy must have thought how perfect it would be to escape the noise and bustle of the city to such bucolic peace – Charles, she thought, had made the right choice in returning to the pastoral life that their great-grandfather, Sam Denton, had left behind him in Hotham in 1820.

A farmhouse tea of home-made pie, freshly-baked scones and jam, raspberry tart with thick cream straight from the dairy, Mrs. Dunning's fruity cake, and cups of the hot, strong tea that Dorothy so loved. A none-too-strenuous game of 'pat-ball' with the boys on the the grass court behind the farm house, a stroll down to the village with its picture-postcard appeal, where in summer local artists came with their canvas and easel to paint the village pond and the old cottages, and soon the afternoon had gone. Before they left, a gift of eggs, butter and a plump young capon pressed on them by Mrs. Dunning. Then Charles and Massey Dunning drove them back in the gathering twilight to Beverley for the train to Hull, to end a perfect day in the country.

Went to City v Newcastle on Hull Fair Day 1910 - City lost 3 - 1.

Hull City always had an attractive home fixture on Hull Fair Saturday. The crowds came to town for the fair, and the 'gate' at Anlaby Road. was usually the best of the season. Newcastle were old rivals – it was said (by Hull folk) that their supporters brought their own beer with them, Hull Brewery ale being too strong for them. There would certainly be a few fights before the night was out, so they also took the precaution of bringing either their Chief Constable, or a senior police officer with them, to arrange bail for those who got into trouble.

1910 was the beginning of Dorothy's interest in football. Jabez bought season tickets for the family, and Dorothy sat in the stand with either her father or her brothers most Saturdays – she even watched the Reserves' games. The game had caught on in Hull, despite the counter attraction of a successful Rugby League team across the road at the Boulevard. In that year some opponents unfamiliar to today's followers of the game appeared at Anlaby Road – Glossop, Leicester Fosse, Gainsborough, Clapton, and Leeds City. 1910/11 was a good season for the Tigers with victories over West Bromwich 5-1, Stockport 4-1, Barnsley 5-1, Leicester Fosse 5-1, Birmingham 4-1, Burnley 3-0, and Sheffield Wednesday 3-0. But promotion to Division One eluded them, as it has done ever since.

Football had become a professional game, but the talented amateur could still hold his own. In 1906 the captain of the Corinthians, international forward Gordon Wright, signed for Hull City, but, as a schoolmaster at Hymers College with Saturday morning classes, he could only play in home matches – the possibility of the Headmaster releasing him from Saturday morning duties to travel to away games would have been out of the question. When the *Hull Daily Mail* sports reporter asked Wright how he liked playing for the Tigers, he loftily conceded, 'They are good fellows, and they play very hard.'

Two of Hull City's best known players at the time were the brothers Tommy and Andy Browell. They lodged in Selby Street, and, on their way back from a morning's training at the ground, often stopped by the

Dentons' front garden gate to chat to Dorothy and Nellie in their broad Durham accents.

Football pools had not yet appeared on the scene in 1910, but the competition run by the *Hull Daily Mail* each week was obviously a forerunner. The weekly prize of £10 was a far cry from Littlewood's £1 million winners, but as no money was allowed to be staked on the *Mail's* free competition, forecasting the results of football matches (soccer and rugby mixed) was not then the big business it has since become.

Father, Ted and I went to the pictures at the Princes Hall, November 17th 1910.

1910 was the year that the cinema in Hull came into its own. Up to that time films had first been seen in the bioscopes at the fair grounds, and later as part of the programme at the theatres and music halls. With the technical improvements in cinema photography, and the growing popularity of the entertainment, a number of hastily converted cinemas had sprung up in city centre shops and church halls. But in 1910 the Princes Hall became Hull's first purpose-built cinema on the site of a Baptist Church in George Street. First the bodies had to be removed from church vaults and the old building demolished; the cinema which took its place cost £10,000 to build.

The Princes Hall was a splendid affair capable of seating 1,500 people on plush tip-up chairs. As an advertising stunt, the management offered two free seats each week for the first person to spot a deliberate mistake in the programme. The full-length feature film had not yet made its appearance, and the programme Dorothy watched that evening would have been a number of short factual or comedy films. The audience was no longer permitted to sit in pitch darkness – new safety laws required management to install subdued lighting. A lady pianist, seated below the screen, played appropriate music to suit the mood, such as *Hearts and Flowers* during the romantic scenes, or *The Light Cavalry* overture to liven up the action.

There was a period when cinemas mushroomed overnight and disappeared just as quickly, but the Princes Hall survived until after the Second War and had the distinction of being the last cinema in Hull to install 'Talkies' in the early 30's.

*Dorothy's Aunt
Jinnie Fenner.*

*Elsie, the eldest of the
Fenner girls.*

*Gertie Fenner,
Dorothy's
attractive
cousin.*

*Edward Ernest Denton - 'Teddie' -
as a small boy around 1906.*

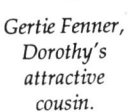

*Max Hans Peter Christian Theede,
1910: 'Cod-eyed Max'.*

1911

Aunt Jinnie, Nellie and I went to the Kinemacolour Jan 16th 1911.

After the success of the Princes Hall, a second new cinema appeared on Anlaby Road on Christmas Eve, 1910. It was the Kinemacolour, which in later years became familiar to Hull's cinema-goers as the Regent. Smaller than the Princes Hall, it featured, as its name suggests, the latest sensation, films in colour. Colour films were an innovation introduced by an American entrepreneur, and it was the only cinema in the city licensed to use his new process. A report in the *Hull Daily Mail* tells us what audiences got for their money, 3d, 6d, and 1/- (with afternoon tea provided in the shilling seats):

'Since the opening of the Kinemacolour Palace on Anlaby Road, people have had the opportunity of witnessing the wonders of natural colour kinematography. This week's programme consists of about 5,000 feet of film of all round excellence. The new process confers upon the week's films perfection.

'As applied to the film, *The Elite of the Canine World*, a remarkable picture of the various animals is produced. A joy to the eye are the pictures of the St. Bernard dog and the Scotch collie dog. The audience did not fail to show their appreciation of the film, *Choice Bouquets*, to which the kinemacolour process was applied – chrysanthemums, carnations, poppies, marigolds and sun-flowers were shown in their actual hue.

'Another fine picture screened in the Kinemacolour machine is *Rough Sea at Santa Lucia* showing sea and surf in perfect colours. The film, *The Last of the Saxons*, a film 902 feet in length, is brimful of interest from start to finish. Those who pay a visit to this place should not fail to see *The Telephone* – 665 feet of this film passes the lens. In brief, a cat overturns a lamp and ignites a table in the house. The wife and child, who are in bed at the time, summon the fire brigade by telephone. The husband is in a club and arrives on the scene in time to see his wife and child rescued.

'Free teas are served to all in the shilling seats, and smoking is permitted.'

Went with Father and Nellie to hear Sousa at the City Hall, February 27th 1911.

John Philip Sousa, the 'March King', and his wonderful band came to Hull during his farewell tour of Britain in 1911. A great showman, as well as the composer of some of the finest marches ever written, Sousa drew wildly enthusiastic audiences wherever he appeared. The City Hall was packed on the night, hundreds being unable to get a seat, and the *Hull Daily Mail* described the scene:

'It was a subdued Sousa – a super Sousa, who dealt out so generous a programme at the City Hall. It was a Sousa in his farewell humour – Sousa of the latter years with nothing in the way of the whimsicality and contortion. Beyond his characteristic shoulder-to-hip swing with both hands, and his intimate initiation of a cadenza on the reeds with his flexible fingers, Sousa was represssed, restrained, and English enough in his methods.

'His band was of course, a "big bit to bite off", with its five ranks of woodwind on the left, and its battery of brass on the right, with its horns in an acute state of elephantiasis, uplifting mouths to the electric chandeliers threatened to swallow the place... It was not to be wondered that the heart of the great audience was filled with exultancy and excitement when Sousa hurled these effects at them with a mighty and ungrudging hand, but to crown all was the episode when his half-dozen trombones and six cornets and four flutes made their way to the front of the platform in an encore march, and fairly blew the souls out of the people in front. It was a great and moving moment, and one long sigh of "Gee" went up from the brave and the fair in their serried thousands.

'This Sousa tour was a wonderful performance in itself. It commenced in January at the London Queen's Hall, and in that month Sousa and his band filled thirty engagements. This month Sousa has visited thirty-three towns in England, Ireland and Scotland. On Sunday his band played at Scarborough, yesterday afternoon at York, and yesterday evening here. Today it is at Grimsby in the afternoon and Lincoln in the evening, and after a visit to Oxford, it departs for South Africa, Australasia, and across America. Here is a Yankee lead in strenuousness with a vengeance. But still Sousa was not too pressed for time or patience to respond again and again to vociferous plaudits last night. Every item on the programme was enthusiastically applauded -

Third Symphony – Les Preludes – Listz.
El Capitain and Hobomoko – Sousa
Dwellers of the Western World – Sousa
Welsh Rhapsody – German

The Old Cloister Clock – Kinkel
Has anybody here seen Kelly?
Stars and Stripes – Sousa
Federal – Sousa
Washington Post – Sousa
Manhatten Beach – Sousa
Slavonic Rhapsody – Freidmann.'

Went to City v Bolton on Sat. 7th Jan 1911. Drew 1 - 1 and at night went to the Grand Cafe with Max Theede.

Went to Palace with Max T. Jan 27th, Victoria Monks.

Sat 11th Feb. Went to Grand Cafe with Max T.

Went to Field's Cafe with M.T. Sat 25th Feb. 1911.

Went with Max to 'The Girl on the Train', Monday 3rd April.

Went to Kinemacolour with Max Tues April 4th.

Kinemacolour with Max and Town at night, May 12th.

Saturday, Max's birthday. Went to Kin. in the afternoon and at night Princes Hall.

Went to London May 27th for five days'.

    Max Hans Peter Christian Theede, who pronounced his name 'Taydee', came into Dorothy's life early in 1911. They met, I believe, through Murie Middlebrook, Dorothy's German-speaking friend, and Max soon won his way into her heart. From his photograph one would judge him to be a very ordinary looking young man, round faced and boyish in appearance, and with those pale blue eyes which earned him from Dorothy's brothers the cruel but apt nickname of 'Cod-eyed-Max'. But foreigners seem always to have had an attraction for English girls, and no doubt Max's *Küsse die Hände* manners had a charm which Dorothy found lacking in English boys. In 1911 this young man, a native of the city of Flensburg on the German/Danish border, was working in Hull for the Deutches Kohlen Depot, a German company which bought British coal for the bunkering of German ships.

It was not to be long before England and Germany were at war with each other, but in 1911 there was little obvious signs of animosity between them. The Englishman's popular image of the German of those days was of the archetypal, red-faced, cornet player in the German bands in the park, or of a corpulent man in *lederhosen*, sinking large steins of lager and eating plates of sausages – the music-halls treated the German as a figure of fun. Max, of course, did not fit into either of these patterns. Exactly what he was up to in England in those days before the Great War is a matter for conjecture, but British Intelligence seems to have had its suspicions. When Max returned hastily to the Fatherland in the summer of 1914, Dorothy was visited by an officer of the counter-espionage services and closely questioned about the activities of her German friend.

But in 1911 Max Theede was an agreeable companion at the theatre or cafe, and was welcomed into the Denton home. A well-educated young man, he spoke English well, and through him Dorothy learned something of the German culture and language. There had been a fair-sized colony of Germans living in Hull in the early years of the century, many of them in long-established businesses in the city, but when war broke out there was an hysterical reaction against them. Those who had not returned to Germany or been interned, had to put up with threats, and in many cases, physical violence from a certain section of the population. Many of the shopkeepers of German origin, even though naturalised British subjects, had their windows broken, and some attempted to escape persecution by changing their names: the family of Hohenrein, pork butchers in Waterworks Street, adopted the name of Ross.

Dorothy pondered for many years over Max's fate for she never heard from him again. She felt sure that he must have died in the war, but, as far as I know, she never made any attempt to find out whether such had been the case. However, in researching details of Dorothy's contemporaries for this book, I discovered that Max had come safely through the war and, like Dorothy, had married late. His wife was a

Danish girl. After the birth of their daughter Edith in 1924, they had all moved to Denmark, but I was unable to trace any of Max's descendants.

In Dorothy's ill-fated love affair with Max may lie a clue to her life in the years between 1914 when Max left her, and her marriage in 1921 to my father. The Great War decimated a generation of young Englishmen, and wiped out the marriage prospects of a million young women like Dorothy. Of the many men she must have met in those seven years, none were to become her husband, and she must have feared that her chances of marriage were gone.

I think she gave her heart completely to Max – she mentioned him in almost every entry in her diary from January 1911 until her last one . . .

Went to London, May 27th

Did she go with Max? A few days later she became 21, an independent woman, and she kept her diary no longer.

POSTSCRIPT

On 23 October 1920 Cyril Edwin Parcell wrote in Dorothy's autograph album the lines of a trite little couplet:
'This world that we're a living in is mighty hard to beat,
We find a thorn with every rose, but ain't the roses sweet.'
She had met him that summer, a good looking 27-year-old ship's officer with the Ellerman's Wilson Line. In 1920 he was engaged on short trips between Hull and the Continent, and he courted her between the weekly runs to Antwerp, Ghent and Hamburg, posting her romantic picture postcards whenever his ship reached port. She kept every one of them in an album.

They were married the following year at Trinity Church in Bridlington, and I was born in March, 1922; my brother Ian was born the following year. Dorothy's and Cyril's marriage lasted for 17 years until 1938 when Cyril died after a long and distressing illness. He was only 44-years-old. Dorothy outlived him by 30 years, dying at Bridlington in 1968, just short of her 78th birthday.

And her sister Nellie's marriage was all too brief; in the War she had married Arnold Silvester, a captain in the East Yorkshire Regiment, leaving Hull in the 1920s when Arnold's job took him to the Midlands. Their sons, Arnold jun. and Peter, were born in 1920 and 1926. In 1932 Nellie's husband contracted pneumonia and the doctors were unable to save him; he too died a young man at the age of 42. Nellie returned to Hull, while the boys remained in boarding school in the South, Arnold later working all his life for Fenners. Nellie died in 1965 at the age of 71.

Charles Robert, the Dentons' elder son, survived the Great War, despite contracting rheumatic fever in Egypt and being invalided out of the East Riding Yeomanry. After the war he married Dorothy Briggs, the daughter of a Beverley agricultural merchant, and farmed most of his life at Bishop Wilton on the edge of the Yorkshire Wolds. They had one son, Kenneth, born in 1921, who suffered from epilepsy and who died by his own hand in 1949. Dorothy (Dord) Denton died in 1966, and Charles, the longest living of the Dentons, reached 79 before he passed away in 1971.

Edward Ernest Denton, the youngest child, remained a bachelor for most of his life. After his mother's death in 1916 he went to live with his Aunt Kate, in Bridlington, working for a few years on his own account as a fish merchant, but when his father died in 1927 he gave up his business, and lived through the twenties and thirties on a small private income. He served in the R.A.F. in World War II, earning a Mention in Despatches for bravery during an attack on his airfield. He married late in life to Jennifer Copley, a lady from the West Riding, and spent his last years in Filey, where he died in 1975 in his mid-70's, and Jenny died within a few months of him.

Jabez Denton served the the Yorkshire Insurance Company all his working life and retired in 1926. Clara had died in 1916, and Jabez remarried in 1922 to Lilian Willingham, I think to avoid being left on his own when Dorothy married. His retirement was, however, a brief one and he died shortly after he ceased work.

Wedding of Dorothy Denton, 1921.